D0883598

CALGARY PUBLIC LIBRARY

MAR − − 2006

Teenagers Guide To The Beatles

Zane Lalani

AverStream Press

Teenagers Guide To The Beatles. Copyright © 2005 Zane Lalani.
All rights reserved. No part of this publication may be reproduced in
any form except by a reviewer in connection with a review.

Published by AverStream Press
www.averstreampress.com, Tampa, FL

Lalani, Zane
        Teenagers Guide To The Beatles
        ISBN 0-96587407-9
        1. Beatles - Juvenile nonfiction. 2. Juvenile music popular

Printed in the United States of America.

Cover photograph by John Dominis/Time & Life Pictures/
Getty Images. Used with permission.

Graphic Design by NA Designs, Tampa, FL

To my daughter
Riyana

Contents

Contents

(continued)

Contents

(continued)

Contents

(continued)

Foreword

By Eloise Costello

Twisting and Shouting with the Beatles

The 1960s decade started out so ordinary, but closed with a collective: "Wow, what an amazing trip! I'm glad I bought *that* ticket to ride!" I was a fourteen-year-old high school freshman in 1964, the perfect age for the Beatles' arrival into my life. I suppose I can sum up my experience in two words, "Beatlemania rules!" All the way from England, from "across the pond," the Beatles were wild, talented, and charismatic. I may not remember all the details, but I will never forget the emotions. They were unique in so many ways, from the tips of their moptop

9

haircuts to the depths of their original music style. Besides, they were singing just to *me*-always!

My first summer with John, Paul, George, and Ringo was a memorable one. My friends and I listened incessantly to *Introducing the Beatles* and *Meet the Beatles*, their first American albums. We studied every note, lyric, and harmony and still we couldn't get enough of it. The best experience that summer of 1964 was the ecstasy of seeing the Beatles up close and personal in *A Hard Day's Night*. I had chills and thrills when they appeared before me larger than life, on the big screen, revealing their personalities and performing for, you guessed it--*me!*

I was the luckiest teenager in the summer of 1965 when my cousin, Bobby, presented me with tickets to the Shea Stadium concert. I had spectacular seats in the Press Box section. The Fab Four might have looked liked little specks out there on second base, but I didn't care. When the reality hit me that I was breathing the same air as my idols, I went crazy, yelling and screaming with emotions I didn't know I had. I am positive that all the Beatles winked at *me* that day.

As the 1960s progressed, I graduated high school and went to college. I took the Beatles with me everywhere I went. I collected all the Beatles albums, savoring every nuance of every song. My favorite album is *Rubber Soul*. I collected all the magazines with Beatles pictures I could afford to buy. My favorite all time Beatles song is "In My Life," and my second favorite song is "Hey Jude." I attest that every morning in the fall of 1968, I woke up to "Hey Jude" playing on my radio. There is no doubt that the Beatles were singing it just for *me*.

Can you tell I was living in bliss and in my own bubble of excitement during Beatlemania? That's the way it was for the many of us who followed the Beatles' music and personal lives so intimately that we felt that we knew them. I guess we just wanted to hold their hands. Today when I hear a Beatles song I am transported back to my youth, and to heartfelt warm memories. I feel fortunate having lived during Beatlemania. Now that we have entered the 21st century, I am proud because *my* Beatles have proven to the world just how powerful and enduring their legacy is for all generations and for many more in the future. You're fortunate, too. Your ticket to ride is just beginning, so get on board the one after 909. I've got a feeling that you will enjoy the Beatles eight days a week just like the fans of the 1960s. And, if you listen carefully, you will realize that the Fab Four are singing their songs just for *you*.

Paul McCartney

John Lennon

George Harrison

Ringo Starr

1

Meet the Beatles

Teenagers' life in pre-Beatlemania Liverpool

Located at the mouth of the River Mersey in northwest England, Liverpool in the 1950s was a small industrial port city with a reputation of being an impoverished and fairly tough place to live. Despite this reputation, Liverpool was a cosmopolitan city with its share of middle class and affluent neighborhoods. Bureaucrats, aristocrats, and business institutions in London generally ignored and looked down on this part of the country. It was easy to identify Liverpudlians by their unique accent and dialect (and it is still today).

"What existed on the banks of the Mersey between 1958 and 1964 was exciting, energetic and unique, a magical time when an entire city danced to the music of youth."

Bill Harry, publisher of *Mersey Beat* and a friend of the Beatles.

Liverpool, a vital seaport bringing in much needed supplies during World War II, had been subjected to substantial bombings. Parts of the city were still in disrepair in the mid-1950s as the first post-war generation of teenagers was carving out a very different life from what its parents experienced. Teenagers in Liverpool went to the movies, dances, shopped, listened to music, watched television, and always looked for ways to earn a bit of pocket money to support their lifestyle. Then there were the rebellious teenaged boys with their greased hair swept back, commonly known as Teddy boys or Teds, many just looking to cause trouble. While this scenario was not much different than in the rest of western world, teenagers in the mid-1950s Liverpool were embarking on a phenomenon, unlike anywhere else in the world that launched many local musicians and singers to international fame.

In the mid-1950s, a British artist called Lonnie Donegan popularized skiffle music with teenagers in Britain. Skiffle music, which originated in the southern United States, is a type of folk music with the influence of jazz and the blues. Using homemade or improvised instruments such as a washboard, tea-chest bass, cigar-box fiddle, or a comb, it presented a very unique sound. Since the instruments were very cheap, a large number of teenagers took to playing skiffle music in Liverpool.

While American music like country & western, the blues, jazz and folk were generally popular in Liverpool, rock and roll became the predominant music for teenagers by the late 1950s. American artists such as Elvis Presley, Buddy Holly and the Crickets, and Little Richard were quite popular and influential as were British artists like Cliff Richard and the Shadows. Many teenagers listened to Radio Luxembourg, which was based in Europe, on small, cheap transistor radios as it was the only radio station that played music they admired so much. Records were selling well, but they really loved listening to the music played live.

The local live music scene in Liverpool was burgeoning to a much greater extent than anywhere in Britain, or elsewhere in the world for that matter. Liverpool, for the size of the city, was in a class by itself as Merseyside teenagers by the thousands packed dozens of large and small social clubs that opened to accommodate this movement. Hundreds of bands formed and they played anywhere they could, including churches, theatres, social halls and private parties. Competition among the bands was fierce. Each band had its own legion of adoring fans. Each band tried to outperform the others. This healthy rivalry compelled some bands to develop creative and innovative techniques and adopt their own style of rock and roll. Soon a whole new, fresh sound surfaced that eventually became known as the Mersey sound or Mersey beat. Out of these bands, the Beatles emerged.

The local and national media ignored this phenomenon. This prompted a teenager, Bill Harry, to launch a new local music publication called *Mersey Beat,* which became very popular among teenagers. According to Bill, "What existed on the banks of the Mersey between 1958 and 1964 was exciting, energetic and unique, a magical time when an entire city danced to the music of youth."

John Winston Lennon

John was born on October 9, 1940 in Liverpool to Julia and Alfred Lennon. Alfred, a steward on a ship, was seldom home and rarely kept in touch with his family. When John was five, his mother's sister Mimi, convinced Julia that John would better off living with her and her husband, John's Uncle George. Since they lived in a very nice middle class neighborhood, Aunt Mimi felt that John would have a stable life with them. Shortly after that, Julia divorced Alfred and John didn't see his father for many years. By the time he was a teenager, John had shown a great deal in of talent in art. He also loved to read and write. One of his favorite books was *Alice in Wonderland.* He dreamed of becoming an artist and writing poetry. His mother was also quite artistic and encouraged his creativity. When he was older, John went to the Liverpool College of Art.

Uncle George died when John was fourteen. Despite Aunt Mimi's strict disciplinary rule, John was frequently in trouble as he was very disruptive in school, which resulted in poor grades. He tried to be tough like a Ted and occasionally got into brawls. Like the rest of the teenagers in Liverpool, he listened to a lot of music, especially American rock and roll. His mother taught him to play the banjo and he soon got his first guitar. He played it like a banjo until he learned how to do it correctly. He wasn't too serious about the guitar at first and nearly gave it up. It took him a couple of years to learn as he taught himself how to play it properly.

He joined with friends and formed a band called the Quarry Men. It was named after his elementary school, Quarry Bank Grammar School. The group played a variety of music including Skiffle, country and western as well as rock and roll. They took every opportunity to play in front of an audience - usually for free. They entered contests, played at parties and church events. When John was eighteen, a drunk driver killed his mother as she attempted to catch a bus. His mother's death profoundly affected John and music became his solace.

James Paul McCartney

Born June 18, 1942 to James and Mary McCartney in Liverpool, Paul's fondest memories as a child were watching his father play the piano at home. When his father was young, he played in a jazz band and his passion for music was passed on to his children. Paul and his younger brother, Mike, had a very stable family life. They lived in a modest home in a middle class neighborhood. Paul was fairly quiet as a child and did quite well at school. He enjoyed playing the piano. He tried piano lessons, but ended up teaching himself just like his father. He never learned to read or write music.

When Paul was just fourteen, his mother died from cancer. With the support of relatives, the family coped with the tragedy and managed to carry on. By that time, Paul's interest in music had become very strong. His father gave him a trumpet for his birthday. He played it for a while, but also wanted to sing and couldn't do both at the same time. For that reason, Paul traded in the trumpet for a guitar. Since he was left handed, he taught himself to play it upside down and got very good at it.

A friend of Paul's invited him to come to a church fete where his friend, John Lennon was playing with a band called the Quarry Men. Paul had seen John around town, but avoided him because John looked quite tough. Paul met John that day. He never imagined that he would ever become friends with him.

George Harold Harrison

The youngest of the four Beatles, George Harrison, was born on February 25, 1943 in Liverpool to Harold and Louise Harrison. He had two older brothers and an older sister. He lived in a modest home in a working class neighborhood. He loved playing sports and enjoyed listening to his parents' records. When George was about twelve, he became quite ill and spent several weeks in the hospital. Shortly after that, he decided he wanted to learn to play the guitar and bought a very cheap one from a schoolmate. Unfortunately, curiosity got the best of George, and when he took the guitar apart to see how it worked, he couldn't put it back together! It wasn't until a year later that his brother fixed it, but the guitar wasn't quite the same. His father played the guitar when he was younger to earn some extra money when he wasn't working. His father arranged for a friend of his to give George guitar lessons. George loved playing the guitar and spent hours practicing.

George attended Liverpool Institute and met Paul McCartney on the bus to school. They found a common interest in music. At that time, Paul had the trumpet and they began to get together and practiced playing their instruments. His interest in music continued to grow as he listened to new music coming from America and what was played on Radio Luxembourg. George had become quite skillful with the guitar by the time he was just fourteen.

Ringo Starr

Ringo was born as Richard Parkin on July 7, 1940 in Liverpool to Richard and Elsie Parkin. He had no siblings. They were quite poor. He grew up in a very tough neighborhood and quickly learned to become a very fast runner in order to avoid getting caught and beaten up by Teddy boys. His parents split up when he was three and his mother remarried. When he was older, his great-grandmother remarried and took the name Starkey. Ringo decided to change his last name to Starkey. When he was a teenager playing in a band, he got the nickname Ringo because of all the rings he wore on his fingers. He thought that Ringo Starkey didn't quite sound right for an entertainer, so he cut last name in half and added an extra 'r' to make it Starr.

Ringo was quite a sickly child spending a lot of time in the hospital with variety of health issues and missed quite a bit of school. Fortunately he outgrew most of his health problems as he got older. He worked at a variety of jobs as a teenager and took a keen interest in music, particularly in the American blues. He even thought about moving to America so he could play with American musicians.

Ringo had taken interest in playing drums and used items like biscuit tin cans to practice. He received a drum set for Christmas, but couldn't play at home due to the loud noise. He soon joined a local band and they practiced wherever they could. The band played for free at weddings and other events just to get a chance to play in front of an audience. As Ringo improved, he began to play with more experienced bands and joined a very popular band called Rory Storm and the Hurricanes. Ringo got to be known as one of the best drummers in Liverpool which was quite a feat considering the large number of bands in Liverpool at that time.

2

Before They Were Fab

John Meets Paul

July 6, 1957, is etched in Beatles history as a significant day, as it was the day when John met Paul. A mutual friend invited Paul to see the Quarry Men perform at a church fete. They met after the performance and hit it off. Paul impressed John with his guitar and singing skills and the fact that Paul knew all the lyrics of a song called "Twenty Flight Rock." Knowing guitar chords, how to tune a guitar, and words to songs was very impressive at that time. The Quarry Men had formed due to friendship rather than talent, but John wanted to make the band better. He saw that Paul was very talented and considered asking Paul to join the group. John was a bit apprehensive as he was the leader and wondered if Paul joined the band, it might threaten his leadership. He also knew, however, that Paul would make the band better. Finally, John asked Paul to join through a band-mate and changed the course of popular music forever.

The band continued to play at church events and dances. John and Paul began to spend a lot of time together practicing and writing songs, essentially forming a "Lennon-McCartney" alliance; to the dismay of other members of the group. It wasn't long before Paul introduced George to John. Being quite young, John didn't take him too seriously, but was impressed with his guitar skills. George eventually became part of the group. It wasn't long before John, Paul and George became the nucleus of the Quarry Men. They practiced at each other's homes frequently and were already trying their hand at writing their own songs.

When John's mother died, his friendship with Paul grew stronger since Paul had gone through a similar tragedy just a few years before and understood what John was going through. By the summer of 1958, the skiffle craze was fading as rock and roll took precedence and grew in influence. As the year progressed, the Quarry Men slowly drifted apart as squabbles within the group took its toll. Interest in the group was waning, as everyone was busy with other activities and essentially quit performing. John was spending a lot of time with his new girlfriend, Cynthia Powell, a fellow student at his art school.

The Casbah & Jacaranda

By 1959, the music scene in Liverpool was burgeoning and teenagers by the thousands packed dozens of large and small social clubs that opened to accommodate the trend. One of these clubs was the Casbah Coffee Club in the cellar of a large Victorian house owned by Mona Best. Prior to the opening of the club, the scheduled band cancelled and it turned out that George had also been playing in that band. He introduced John and Paul to Mona. She took a liking to them and offered them a weekly Saturday night appearance. Just before opening night, the club still needed work before it opened. John, Paul and George pitched in to help paint the club. The Quarry Men with John, Paul and George opened with no drummer. A disagreement over money with Mona ended their stint at the Casbah just a few weeks later.

The Quarry Men decided to change their name to Johnny and the Moondogs because many of the popular groups had names like that: the lead singer's name followed by "and the such-and-such." They were still without a regular drummer and had difficulty finding one. Unlike other instruments, drums were costly and all the drummers they knew were already in bands. They also needed a bass guitarist and convinced Stuart (Stu) Sutcliff, a friend of John's from art school, to buy one and join the band. He did, but was only just learning to play it. By now, hundreds of bands had formed and it was very competitive. Without a regular drummer, they had difficulty getting many opportunities to play at clubs, although Paul would occasionally play the drums. To keep busy, they entered contests, even those in neighboring cities. They frequented a popular club called the Jacaranda, hoping to get a chance to play there. They even managed to practice there occasionally. A popular band, Rory Storm and the Hurricanes, often played there with Ringo Starr as their drummer.

Finally, Alan Williams, the owner of the Jacaranda, got them an audition with a national music promoter who was looking for several bands to accompany major stars on

Beatle Bits

Over the course of two years, the Quarry Men had several different band members. Some of the key members were:

John Lennon	Len Garry
Pete Shotton	Ivan Vaughn
Colin Hanton	Nigel Whalley
Eric Griffiths	Paul McCartney
Rod Davis	George Harrison

During their tour with Johnny Gentle, they changed their names to:

Paul: Paul Ramon
George: Carl Harrison
Stu: Stuart de Stael
John: Long John.

Van tales

They had to endure a lot of difficulties with their old, graffiti covered van especially on tours. Once, a small rock smashed the windshield of the van. They ended up driving 200 miles without a windshield in the middle of winter in Scotland. On another occasion, the van skidded off the highway, down a slope and turned over to its side. Fortunately, they were not injured. They straightened the van, pushed it up the slope and went on their way.

national tours. They were told get a new name. John and Stuart came up with Long John and the Silver Beetles presumably to emulate Buddy Holly and the Crickets. They ended up shortening the name to the Silver Beetles for the purposes of the audition. John came up with the idea of changing one of the letters 'e' in beetles to an 'a' and the name was ultimately shortened it to the Beatles.

The Silver Beatles found a temporary drummer and auditioned for the national promoter. The Beatles were concerned with the lack of Stuart's ability to play the bass guitar, so he was asked to keep his back to the audience as much as possible so no one would notice him playing incorrectly. The promoter selected them to accompany a not-so-famous star, Johnny Gentle and they had to spruce themselves up by wearing matching outfits. Despite this, they were ecstatic and went on a tour around Scotland with him. The tour was very demanding as the means of travel and the accommodations were substandard, but they were still delighted at having the chance. When they returned to Liverpool, they got to play occasionally at the Jacaranda and a few other places with the help of Alan, who was acting as their unofficial manager. The Beatles had become used to playing in tough clubs and usually managed to escape violent patrons. In one incident, however, Stuart did suffer a bloody head injury. Fortunately he managed to recover fairly quickly.

Hamburg, Germany

Bruno Koschmider, the owner of several nightclubs in Hamburg, Germany, was looking for British groups and struck a deal with Alan to get some Liverpool bands to play in his clubs. Alan offered the Beatles the chance to go to Hamburg and they jumped at the opportunity since Liverpool was bursting with bands. The only hitch was they needed a drummer immediately. Fortunately, Pete Best, Mona's son from the Casbah, was interested and joined the band as the fifth Beatle. Finally, the Beatles had a complete band and headed to Germany in the summer of 1960.

The lack of proper travel documents almost got them turned back at the border, but Alan managed to convince the authorities to let them in. When the Beatles arrived in Hamburg, they found out that they were going to play and live in a seedy and tough part of town saturated with nightclubs. Other British bands were already playing in some of these clubs including Tony Sheridan, and Rory Storm and the Hurricanes. Their living conditions were sub-standard. They were put up in a very small room behind the movie screen in a movie theater, across the road from the Indra Club where they were scheduled to perform. Unlike Liverpool, the music scene in Hamburg was largely relegated to a small part of town and catered primarily to adults.

Despite the circumstances, they looked forward to playing for an extended period in one club. Unlike their short performances in Liverpool, here they played for several hours every night, often into the small hours of the morning. Just like Liverpool, some of the patrons were quite belligerent and fights would often break out in the club. To satisfy the tough crowd, the club owner wanted the Beatles to be more outlandish in their performances. It didn't take long for wildness to emerge from some of the Beatles. While John, Paul and George showed streaks of wildness, Stu and Pete were quite reserved. After a slow start, the Beatles began to develop a fan base and were improving their stage presence as well as sharpening their musical skills. Unfortunately, the Indra was shut down shortly after it opened due to complaints from neighbors about the excessive noise from the music.

Koschmider booked them at the Kaiserkeller, one of

his other clubs. Rory Storm and the Hurricanes were the top draw there. Playing in the same club, Ringo Starr got to know the Beatles better. In fact, when the Beatles got an opportunity to have a couple of songs recorded at an amateur studio, Ringo played drums for them for the first time because Pete wasn't available at that time. Pete spent a lot of time by himself, so Ringo filled in a few times for Pete. There was quite a bit of competition between Rory Storm and the Beatles. Both bands played long hours every day and tried to outdo each other, which helped the Beatles improve their skills. Playing for long hours also helped enhance their repertoire and they continuously looked for, and experimented with, new material.

Stu met and fell in love with Astrid Kirchherr, a local photographer who frequently watched the Beatles play. She got the Beatles to pose for photo sessions and some of those photographs have become quite famous. She is also credited for changing their hairstyles, which gave them a unique look for many years. They also began to wear black leather jackets giving them a tougher image. Astrid's mother invited the boys for meals and soon Stu moved into a spare room. Shortly after moving, he got engaged to Astrid.

The Top Ten, a new and larger club, had opened recently and booked British acts including Tony Sheridan. The club owner, Peter Eckhorn, had managed to recruit some bands like Rory Storm and the Hurricanes and other club staff from the Kaiserkeller, which upset Koschmider. The Beatles visited that club frequently and occasionally jammed on stage with Tony Sheridan. Koschmider was not pleased with the Beatles when he heard about it. After a heated argument with him, the Beatles left to play at the Top Ten. They didn't play there for long before George ended up getting deported back to England because he was under the age of eighteen and wasn't allowed to play at these

Above: Posing for Astrid Kirchner in Hamburg. Left to right: Pete Best, George Harrison, John Lennon, Paul McCartney, and Stuart Sutcliff.

Below: Live on stage. Left to right: Paul, Pete, Stuart, George, and John

Ringo Starr before he joined the Beatles.

nightclubs. Previously, he had managed to evade the authorities that frequently checked identification for age at the nightclubs.

The rest of the Beatles continued to perform at the Top Ten, but only for a brief period as Paul and Pete ended up getting deported too. Paul and Pete had been arrested for setting fire to their accommodations. Apparently, while they were packing to move out of the room that Koschmider had rented to them, they got carried away fooling around with matches, resulting in some minor fire damage. Koschmider was furious. Fortunately, he didn't press charges, but turned them over to authorities. They immediately deported them back to England. It happened so quickly that Pete ended up having to leave his drum set behind. John returned to England shortly afterward, but Stu decided to stay behind with Astrid.

Direct from Hamburg: The Beatles

The extraordinary experience in Hamburg had taken its toll on the Beatles. While their music skills and stage presence had improved dramatically, they were mentally and physically exhausted because of the long hours, poor diet, and lack of sleep. They were broke and unsure of their future. Paul even got a job at a factory at the insistence of his father. 1961 was just around the corner and John, Paul, and George had been together for over three years, but it seemed their music careers wasn't going anywhere. They were quite disillusioned. Several days went by before they got in touch with each other. The music scene in Liverpool was hotter than ever and it was inevitable that they would be drawn to it again. John and George, however, had to persuade Paul to continue playing with the group. It wasn't long before Stu returned from Germany and once again, they were ready to perform.

The Cavern Club

Pete's mother offered to let them play at the Casbah again. They also began to play at other small venues. A local club disc jockey, Bob Wooler, managed to get them an appearance at a large, popular dance hall called Litherland Town Hall. The Beatles were promoted as a band from Hamburg, so a lot of patrons thought they were German. Their experience in Hamburg had begun to pay off, as the Beatles were an instant hit with the crowd. The Beatles' sound and highly energetic performance was something not previously seen around there. The stage presence of other bands in Liverpool was fairly reserved in comparison. Also, since Paul was left-handed, he and John used the same microphone when they sang together, producing a visual effect that few groups could imitate. Pete had become a crowd favorite. A promoter, Brian Kelly, signed them up for several performances over the next three months.

Wooler also got them booked at the Cavern Jazz

Club. The owner was persuaded to try rock and roll during the lunch hour. Located in the cellar of a warehouse, the Cavern Club was a small dark place with very little ventilation. When the club was crowded, the dampness level was so high that moisture dripped down from the ceilings and the walls. It occasionally shorted the musical equipment. Despite the inhospitable conditions at the club, the Beatles drew large lunchtime crowds, consisting mostly of young female office and shop workers. These normally mild-mannered girls lined up for blocks to get into the club and turned into a boisterous bunch during the performances. It was here that the Beatles began to develop a real connection to the audience. They told unrehearsed jokes, carried out comical skits, and made off-the-cuff remarks that the crowd appreciated. Competition between bands was intense and every band tried to out do each other by coming up with innovative and creative techniques. The Beatles also began play at the Cavern in the evenings to an even more frenzied crowd. Little did they know that this was just a taste of the mania that would soon be unleashed.

In April 1961, the Beatles returned to Hamburg for a short time to play at the Top Ten Club. George had turned eighteen and Peter Eckhorn, the owner of the Top Ten Club, had managed to get them proper travel and work permits, despite their previous troubles with the law. He provided comfortable accommodations and paid them better, too. They continued playing for long hours, though this time they alternated shows with Tony Sheridan, giving them a bit of a break. They got leather trousers, cowboy boots, and new hairstyles, albeit reluctantly, thanks to Astrid. With Astrid's encouragement, Stu pursued his real interest in art while trying to juggle his time playing with the band. He kept reducing time spent playing with the band and eventually he stopped playing with the band altogether.

Tony Sheridan had just signed with a record label

and asked the Beatles back him on an upcoming recording session. The Beatles, however, had to go by the name "Beat Brothers" because the producer felt it was better suited to the German audience. They backed Tony Sheridan on several songs including "My Bonnie Lies Over the Ocean," which was selected for release as a single. The producer was quite impressed with the Beatles and asked them record a few of their own songs, but he didn't do anything with the recordings and put the tapes away in storage.

The Beatles returned to Liverpool in the summer without Stu, as he decided to remain in Hamburg with Astrid. It was back to the Cavern Club and the other venues as usual for the Beatles. The Beatles needed reliable transportation to get around town and also needed help to look after their equipment. Neil Aspinall, Pete's best friend, had a van and agreed to become their road manager for a small fee.

Bill Harry, who started the *Mersey Beat,* was a friend of John's from art school. The Beatles were promoted heavily in his paper, and in fact, John contributed some of his own writings. They had become well known in the local music circle and in fact were being imitated by many bands. Despite this, it seemed that life for the Beatles had become routine and they were growing restless.

A Cellarful of Noise

Brian Epstein's family owned a small chain of music stores and he managed the location near the Cavern Club. In his autobiography, *A Cellarful of Noise*, Brian recounts how he came to meet the Beatles. A customer requested "My Bonnie Lies over the Ocean," the record in which the Beatles backed Tony Sheridan in Germany. The Beatles weren't listed on the record by name. Brian didn't have the record, but always made an effort to please his customers.

He managed to find the record. Soon other customers were requesting it, so he decided to find out a bit more about the Beatles. Some dispute this account since *Mersey Beat* had been distributed in Brian's store and the Beatles were prominent in the paper. Bill Harry has also stated that he had talked to Brian about the Beatles previously.

In November 1961, Brian went to the Cavern Club to see the Beatles perform. Brian, conservatively dressed, went to the underground teenage hotspot and watched the Beatles perform. He was very impressed with their energetic performance and took an immediate liking to them, despite their rough appearance and wild behavior. He arranged for a meeting with them. Brian and the Beatles related to each other well at the meeting. Shortly after the meeting, the Beatles agreed to let Brian became their official manager, even though he didn't have any prior experience as a band manager. He had made a very good impression on them and they were anxious to start recording the scores of songs that John and Paul had written. Although there were hundreds of bands to pick from in Liverpool, he saw something in the Beatles that other bands didn't have. He also knew that their success hinged upon a recording contract with a major record label and felt that with his contacts in the music industry, he would no trouble getting them a record contract.

Almost immediately, Brian arranged an audition for them just a few days away at Decca Records in London on New Years Day 1962. The Beatles were ecstatic as could be expected. He was also able to get them better venues to perform in for more money. The songs they played at the audition were mostly popular American songs, with just three of their own songs. The Beatles' performance at the audition could be considered average for their potential. In addition to being a bit nervous for such an important event, they weren't quite comfortable in the cold, sterile environment of a recording studio. Beside that, they were up late the previous night celebrating New Year's Eve. Still, they were optimistic as they returned to Liverpool and waited to hear back from the London studio on their decision.

The *Mersey Beat* readers had voted the Beatles as the best group in town. Rory Storm and the Hurricanes were also voted among the top groups. Despite their popularity locally, however, Decca turned the Beatles down. Brian was told that guitar groups were on their way out. Brian attempted to draw interest from other major record labels, but to no avail. Once again, the Beatles had hit a roadblock. As Brian continued to book them into better venues, he felt they needed to clean up their image to fit these settings. Reluctantly, they began to put on suits and ties for some performances as Brian continued his search for a record contract.

In mid-April, they were scheduled to return to Hamburg for a seven-week engagement at a new venue called the Star-Club. As they were preparing to fly down, they received some shocking news. Stu had died of a brain hemorrhage. They were devastated by the news of Stu's death. For the first time, they had to cope with the death of someone their own age. Astrid met the Beatles at the Hamburg Airport and told them that Stu had been having severe headaches for a long time, but no cause had been established. It was suspected that the bloody head injury he received during a skirmish in Liverpool sometime back, might have contributed to his death. The Beatles put on a brave face and performed at the Star-Club for the next seven weeks. Although they managed to continue with their wild and crazy antics, if it wasn't for some good news they received from Brian a couple of weeks later, the engagement would have been a disaster.

Copyright Bill Harry/Mersey Beat Ltd.

Front page of *Mersey Beat* announcing the results of their top bands survey.

"Please send us £10,000"

Brian found himself under a lot of pressure. He was testing his parents' patience by devoting far too much time to the Beatles and not enough to his store. He also felt he was letting the Beatles down by not coming through with his promise of a recording contract. In addition to the expected challenge of finding someone who could envision the potential of the Beatles, Brian faced a negative bias from Londoners towards those from northern England. Since all the major record companies had turned them down, Brian continued his quest for a recording contract by contacting small record companies, but he didn't fare much better. Just when Brian thought he had exhausted every avenue, he was referred to George Martin, head of Parlophone Records. Brian wasn't very optimistic, however, as it was a subsidiary of a large record company called EMI and other EMI subsidiaries had previously turned down the Beatles. Besides, Parlophone was largely known for its comedy records and some rather peculiar acts. Without any other prospects, he decided to contact George Martin.

George Martin met Brian at Abbey Road Studios and listened to the recording made during the Decca audition. Brian described Martin as a "tall, thin, elegant man with the air of a stern but fair-minded housemaster." Although George Martin was not overwhelmed by recordings, he wrote in his autobiography, "there was an unusual sound about them, a certain roughness that I hadn't encountered before." He felt they warranted a further look. George Martin was unaware that every record company that Brian had contacted had turned them down. Brian and George Martin agreed on a recording test as soon as the Beatles returned from Hamburg the following month. Brian was certain that a contract was imminent and immediately sent a telegram to the Beatles and urged them to work on

Beatle Bits

Brian Epstein

Brian Epstein started working at his family's furniture store in Liverpool when he was sixteen. He became a very good salesperson. After a few years at the store, Brian got bored and decided to pursue his dream of becoming an actor. He was accepted at the Royal Academy of Dramatic Art in London. Brian quickly became disenchanted with the acting profession and returned to the family business. The business expanded into selling musical instruments and records and was called North End Road Music Stores (NEMS). Paul's father bought his first piano from Brian's father when Paul was very young. When the family opened additional locations, Brian managed a store near the Cavern Club. He was very interested in music and kept a large selection of records in his store. When Brian became the Beatles manager, he never signed the managing contract. He felt that it gave the Beatles the option to leave him if they weren't happy with him. He was a man of his word.

George Martin

George Martin loved music ever since he was a little boy. During World War II, he joined the British Navy at seventeen. Fortunately, the war was over before he could be sent to battle. He went on to study music at the Guildhall School of Music in London. He became a very good pianist. Jobs were hard to find, so he became a clerk at the BBC Music Library until he got a job at EMI's Parlophone Records division as an assistant producer. Parlophone had a very small budget and produced for lesser-known artists. Within a few years, George Martin was made the head of Parlophone Records. He focused primarily on recording comedy acts and although he was reasonably successful, his sales paled when compared to sales of rock and roll records at other record labels. Then, he signed the Beatles and the rest is history.

Brian Epstein, left and George Martin, right at Abbey Road Studios.

new material. As expected, the Beatles were very excited and in their typical humorous style, they responded by asking Brian to send them £10,000 advance royalties and to order four new guitars.

The Beatles met George Martin at Abbey Road Studios in June 1962 and they hit it off right away. He was most impressed with their engaging personalities, though he found Pete to be very reserved. They already knew about George Martin and were fans of his comedy records. The Beatles played both the usual cover songs and some songs that John and Paul had written including "Love Me Do" and "P.S. I Love You." George Martin felt that the group had real potential, but would have to find new material for them, as he wasn't too impressed with their own songs. He was impressed, however, that the John, Paul and George all sang which was quite unusual then. In those days, most popular groups such as Cliff Richard and the Shadows, had a lead singer with a back up band. During the audition, George Martin looked for a lead singer in the group. He felt that Paul was best suited for the role, but realized that a lead singer would change the nature of the group. He had been successful in experimenting in comedy, so he thought why not experiment in pop music and have them all sing?

George Martin wasn't too pleased with the drumming and decided that since no one sees one play in the studio, he would use his own professional drummer during studio recordings. He told Brian about his decision and that it didn't matter to him who played drums when they were on stage. Brian told the John, Paul and George what George Martin told him. Apparently the other three Beatles had been considering replacing Pete. They told Brian they wanted Ringo since he was one of the best drummers in Liverpool and he had performed with them numerous times when Pete was unavailable. Brian would have to be the one to tell Pete the bad news. He decided to wait for a while.

"I don't like your tie"

Before George Martin offered the Beatles a contract, he traveled to Liverpool to see them perform at the Cavern Club. He saw what Brian had seen: an energetic and electrifying performance that reached the teenage audience like nothing he'd ever seen before. He knew that if he could harness and direct the energy and talent they showed in live performances to a studio setting, he had the makings of a successful group. It was also apparent how well John, Paul and George worked together and that reinforced his idea that he wasn't going to choose a lead singer. He even thought about making a live recording at the Cavern Club to capture the sound in such a setting. He immediately contacted Brian and offered the Beatles a contract.

Despite George Martin's enthusiasm for the Beatles, many at EMI were quite skeptical and some of his colleagues even teased him about them. After all, he had earned a reputation for bringing in odd acts and now he had probably topped it with these unrefined Liverpudlians.

Brian waited another month before he told Pete that the rest of the group wanted him out. Pete was shocked. He didn't see it coming. Neil, Pete's friend and the Beatles road manager, wanted to quit, but Pete talked him out of it. When word got out, many fans protested, since Pete was the favorite especially with teenaged girls. At a gig, some fans got violent and George ended up with a black eye. Even Brian kept a bodyguard for a while until the opposition subsided. Brian had started managing other bands and was able to find a band for Pete to join. John telephoned Ringo with the news and Ringo joined the band shortly afterward. It seems that they had discussed this with Ringo previously and were waiting for the right moment. Around this time, John and his long-time girlfriend, Cynthia, got married in a small, private ceremony.

John Lennon with his new bride, Cynthia.

In September, the Beatles returned to Abbey Road Studios to begin recording. George Martin was unaware that they had replaced Pete and was surprised to see Ringo because he had brought in Andy White, a professional session drummer, for the recording session. He didn't know how well Ringo played and opted to use Andy. That didn't please the Beatles. Ringo thought that he might not continue as a Beatle. George Martin also decided that he would record some songs written by John and Paul. He tried to ease the tension by letting Ringo play the tambourine on "Love Me Do" and then did a second version with Ringo on drums. He found that Ringo was an excellent drummer with a knack for the Beatles style.

George Martin realized that the Beatles were more than just performers. They were multi-talented and he felt that including them in the whole recording process would help their relationship with him, especially in light of the drumming situation. As they sat in the technical control room listening to their recording, George Martin told them to tell him if there was something they didn't like. George looked at him with a straight face and said, "Well, for a start, I don't like your tie." Everyone burst out laughing and it marked the beginning of a close relationship that was about to make pop culture history.

BEATLEMANIA!

It's happening everywhere.. even in sedate Cheltenham

OUT OF THIS WORLD! The strong arm of the law holds back a fan with a bad attack of Beatlemania.

Pictures by Mirror Cameramen Bill Ellmann and Maurice Tibbles.

Out of this world! These are the symptoms of Beatlemania.

The with-it bug bites so hard..

EVERYONE, everywhere is catching it. IT is called Beatlemania.

Earlier this week it swept Sweden.

Last night it hit sedate Cheltenham—traditional home of retired brigadiers, colonels . . . and the Ladies' College.

And if you haven't got it yet, these fantastic pictures show just what Beatlemania can do.

Cheltenham loved it.

The four pop-singing Beatles took the stage of a cinema for two concerts —the start of a five-week British tour.

Screamed

And 1,800 Beatlemaniacs squealed and screamed . . . right through the opening number.

Beatles leader John Lennon, 23, bawled for quiet. It just brought more squeals.

As Lennon and his fellow-Beatles, Paul McCartney, Ringo Starr and George Harrison, struggled manfully on, girls left their seats and rushed to the stage.

Two fans fell into the orchestra pit. The second - house reception was even more ecstatic.

Hundreds stood on their seats, waving coats and umbrellas.

Programmes were thrown on to the stage— with telephone numbers written on them in lipstick. . . .

NOT TO BE MISSED
UNBELIEVABLE
PRICE SLASH
GUARANTEED SWISS MADE
WATCHES AUTOMATIC GOLD
PLATED JEWELLED MOVEMENT

£8'8'0

41 PIECE WILLOW PATTERN CROCKERY SET
89/11

2 WAVE BAND RADIO
MEDIUM/LONG
85/-
10/- DEPOSIT

ENGLISH & OVERSEAS
DIRECT SUPPLY LTD.
ORDERS TO: Dept. No. D44G, 169 Regent St., London, W.1

3

Beatlemania

"Gentlemen, you've just made your first number one record"

On October 4, 1962, "Love Me Do/PS I Love You" was released as a single. Each single record had a song on each side. The first song listed is the main song. The side that the main song is on is referred to as the 'A' side and the other side as the 'B' side. Brian's next task was to get them some publicity and promote 'Love Me Do." It was a challenging task since American releases dominated the national music charts and EMI did very little to promote the Beatles. The *Mersey Beat* was doing a great job in promoting the record, but the daily newspapers paid very little attention to them. Although "Love Me Do" topped the charts in northern England, it only reached number seventeen nationally, dashing the high hopes everyone had for the record. The south, particularly London, was still hard to break into. The Beatles continued performing in the north with ever-increasing popularity and appeared as second or third billing on stops by other acts, including one of their icons, Little Richard. In December, they reluctantly returned to perform at the Star-Club in Hamburg for a short stint since they had agreed to it during their last visit.

When the Beatles returned to Abbey Road Studios in January 1963 for the next recording session, George Martin had selected a song written by another writer to record for their next single since "Love Me Do" didn't top the charts. The Beatles were adamant about selecting one of their own songs. George Martin tersely told them their song had to be very good to be selected for release. Singer-songwriters were virtually unheard of in those days as it was customary that the producers selected songs from professional songwriters for their artists to record and play. John and Paul played "Please Please, Me" for him. After a few modifications, they recorded it. After the recording, George Martin announced through the intercom, "Gentlemen, you've just made your first number one record."

On January 11, 1963 "Please Please, Me/Ask Me Why" was released. Brian teamed up with Dick James, a music publisher who had worked with George Martin previously. This time there was more support for the single since Dick was experienced in music promotions. They also got more support from EMI. The timing of the release was perfect as they were scheduled to appear on national television pop music show called *Thank Your Lucky Stars*. Now the national teenaged audience would see what the Liverpool teenagers were so hysterical about. "Please

Please, Me" began to rise quickly in the national charts. The Beatles also went on tour with Helen Shapiro, a popular teenaged singer, and promoted their record every chance they got. Within a few weeks, "Please Please, Me" became the number one song in the country.

"The darlings of Merseyside"

The Beatles finally attracted the attention of a major London newspaper. Maureen Cleave, a music columnist for the *Evening Standard,* interviewed the Beatles and called them "the darlings of Merseyside." In her column headlined, "Why the Beatles Create All That Frenzy," she wrote, "They don't sound like the Shadows or anybody else for that matter." She added that the girls in Merseyside were "fiercely possessive about their Beatles" and that "they wouldn't buy their first record in case they should become famous and go away to London and leave them."

Brian was inundated with appearance requests for the Beatles. They became frequent guests on radio shows, including *Saturday Club* and *Parade of the Pops*, popular music shows on the British Broadcasting Corporation (BBC), the national radio and television network. They weren't bashful and their charm and humor came across very well. The Beatles' schedule became very demanding and there was no end in sight to their frantic pace of touring. Despite the recent success, they weren't making much money. Many of the tours were booked at a low rate prior to their hit. Still, they enjoyed touring because it got them out of Liverpool. As they traveled the country in Neil's old van, they had their share of mechanical troubles and accidents. However, the hours spent together in a van going from place to place, day after day brought them very close to each other. Touring started to take a toll on Neil's health, so Brian hired Mal Evans, a former Cavern Club employee, to help.

His large size also helped in protecting the Beatles from some of the overly enthusiastic fans.

George Martin was watching the rise of "Please Please, Me" and knew that they needed a long play (LP) album quickly. He recalled their energetic Cavern Club performance and wanted to try and reproduce it in the studio. George Martin was amazed at the number of songs John and Paul had already written and was unaware that they had been writing songs since they were teenagers. Brian had recognized this talent and was letting some of his other acts record their songs. Paul and John were now professional songwriters in their own right and they were only twenty years and twenty-one old, respectively. Dick James, their music publisher, set up a company called Northern Songs through which all of John and Paul's songs would be published under Lennon/McCartney. John and Paul agreed to share the writing credits regardless of who wrote the song. As it was, both contributed quite a bit to each other's songs. This was a historical moment as it set up one of the most prolific song writing teams in history.

Fourteen songs were selected for the new LP, seven by John and Paul, including "I Saw Her Standing There" and "P.S. I Love You." The entire album was recorded in one day, an amazing feat. All four of them had at least one song in which they sang the lead vocals, another thing unheard of at that time. George sang lead on "Do You Want to Know a Secret," a Lennon/McCartney song, while Ringo covered "Boys." "The "Please Please, Me" single was also included, but this time with Ringo on drums. The album, titled after the hit single "Please Please, Me," was released in March and quickly rose to number one nationally.

Above: Front cover of *Please Please Me*.

Below: Back cover of *Please Please Me*.

```
┌─────────────────────────────────────────────────────┐
│ [1] I SAW HER STANDING THERE                         │
│     (McCartney/Lennon)                               │
│ [2] MISERY (McCartney/Lennon)                        │
│ [3] ANNA (GO TO HIM)                                 │
│     (Alexander)                                      │
│ [4] CHAINS (Goffin/King)                             │
│ [5] BOYS (Dixon/Farrell)                             │
│ [6] ASK ME WHY                                       │
│     (McCartney/Lennon)                               │
│ [7] PLEASE PLEASE ME                                 │
│     (McCartney/Lennon)                               │
│ [8] LOVE ME DO (McCartney/Lennon)                    │
│ [9] P.S. I LOVE YOU                                  │
│     (McCartney/Lennon)                               │
│ [10] BABY IT'S YOU (David/Williams/Bacharach)        │
│ [11] DO YOU WANT TO KNOW A SECRET                    │
│      (McCartney/Lennon)                              │
│ [12] A TASTE OF HONEY (Scott/Marlow)                 │
│ [13] THERE'S A PLACE (McCartney/Lennon)              │
│ [14] TWIST AND SHOUT (Medley/Russell)                │
│                                                      │
│ ℗ 1963 ORIGINAL SOUND RECORDINGS MADE BY             │
│ EMI RECORDS LTD.                                     │
│ © 1963 EMI RECORDS LTD.                              │
└─────────────────────────────────────────────────────┘
```

Please Please Me song list

Beatle Bits

The Beatles started recording the album at noon and finished by midnight. Since they had played these songs several times at concerts, they didn't rehearse for the album. The very last song to be recorded was "Twist and Shout" because the song strained John's vocal cords. John's throat hurt for a long time after that recording. It didn't help that they had been recording for several hours before the song and John had a cold.

Jelly babies

In the midst of all this frenzy, Cynthia gave birth to Julian Lennon on April 8, 1963. The frantic pace of the schedule gave John very little time to be with his new son. The next single, "From Me to You/Thank You Girl" was released and quickly reached number one. Having this single reach number one was very important because it established them as legitimate artists and removed any doubts about them as "one hit wonders."

By now Brian was managing several successful Liverpool-based bands and major record companies had taken notice. Their talent scouts were scouring Liverpool for bands with the "Liverpool or Mersey sound." It seemed that the unique Liverpudlian accent was labeled as special music sound. The *Daily Mirror,* a major London newspaper, took notice. In June, the newspaper published a large photograph of three of Brian's most successful bands: the Beatles, Gerry and the Pacemakers, and Billy J. Kramer and the Dakotas with the headline, "13 POP STARS FROM ONE CITY." The paper reported that at that time, the bands occupied three of the top four places in the music charts and the three groups had sold about two million records combined in six months.

Despite this publicity, the Beatles managed to walk around London generally unrecognized which wasn't the case in most of the cities in the north. One day John and Paul were walking in London when they ran into Mick Jagger from a band called the Rolling Stones. He mentioned to them that the Rolling Stones had signed with Decca records (the first record company that turned the Beatles down) and wondered if the Beatles had any songs his band could use. John and Paul were in the midst of writing "I Wanna Be Your Man" for their next LP and thought it would suit the Rolling Stones. So they went with Mick to the

The Beatles, Gerry and the Pacemakers, Billy J. Kramer and the Dakotas having some fun before posing for a photograph for the *Daily Mirror*. From left to right: The Beatles: John Lennon, Paul McCartney, Ringo Starr and George Harrison. Gerry and the Pacemakers: Gerry Marsden, Freddie Marsden, Les Chadwick and Les McGuire. Billy J Kramer and the Dakotas Robin McDonald, Mike Maxfield, Billy J Kramer, Ray Jones and Tony Mansfield. All the groups were managed by Brian Epstein pictured far right.

studio and played some of the song. The Rolling Stones liked it, so John and Paul sat down and finished writing the rest of the song for them in just a few minutes, to the amazement of the band. The song was the first one by the Rolling Stones to make it in the top twenty of the record chart. The Beatles and the Rolling Stones remained close friends ever since.

In August, after hundreds of performances, the Beatles played for the last time at the Cavern Club. They had outgrown the place that had given them some of the best and worst times of their short career. It was the place where Brian and George Martin first saw the Beatles' electrifying and energetic performance and where they perfected the art of playing live, feeding off the response from the fans. Now in some of the larger venues, the incessant screams of the fans overpowered the music and even the Beatles couldn't hear what they were playing. The Beatles were a bit embarrassed playing at some of the places in Liverpool since they had discarded their leather jackets and tough image for suits and ties.

Some over-zealous fans were creating a lot of fuss around the Beatles' homes as well. The telephone was constantly ringing, girls were repeatedly at the door and many slept in the yard hoping to get a glimpse of one of any of the Beatles. Since the Beatles were frequently away from home, their families had to put up with the aggravation. The Beatles had their own irritations to put up with. Getting in and out of venues safely was getting more and more difficult as there were mobs of fans at the entrance. Sometimes they would enter and leave from the side entrances; at other times they would use an underground connector between buildings and enter and exit from the building next door. On one occasion they used the trap door on the roof to get to the next building and made their get away.

The Beatles performing on *Ready, Steady, Go* television show.

Police attempt to control over-zealous Beatles fans.

Beatle Bits

In addition to several television and radio appearances, the Beatles performed in over 200 concerts in 1963. They went on six national tours accompanying other artists including Roy Orbison. As the year progressed, the Beatles became the primary attraction on these tours.

Brian set up an official fan club to manage the mounds of fan mail the Beatles were receiving. An independent fan magazine devoted just to the Beatles, called *Beatles Book* also began to publish. One of the biggest regrets the Beatles had was a comment made by one of them that they liked jelly babies, which are very similar to jelly beans. Frenzied fans began deluge the stage with jelly babies, many dangerously close to hurting them. Despite pleas from the Beatles, the jelly baby craze could not be stopped.

"Yeah, Yeah, Yeah"

The Beatles finally got a chance to take a short break from all the frenzy. Paul and Ringo went to Greece, John and Cynthia went to Paris and George went to the United States of America to visit his sister, Louise, who had moved there. Louise had been in contact with Brian who had been sending her Beatles records. She managed to get her small town radio station to play them. Brian could not convince EMI's sister company in America, Capitol Records, to distribute the Beatles. Therefore a couple of smaller record distributors agreed to distribute the Beatles. Unfortunately, due to a variety of issues, not a lot was done to promote the songs, so the singles did not do well on the record charts. When George returned to Britain, he brought back a large assortment of American records.

"She Loves You/I'll Get You" was released in August and it reached number one in the very first week! The single became the biggest selling record in British history. The chorus, "Yeah, Yeah, Yeah" became synonymous with the Beatles and was quoted frequently by the media. They recorded *With The Beatles*, their second album. It had been decided that there wouldn't be any songs that were released as singles placed on their albums. They felt it cheated the fans if they bought a single and later bought an album with the single on it. There were seven songs written by John and Paul. George wrote "Don't Bother Me," his first one. Ringo sang the lead on "I Wanna Be Your Man."

Some of the major media in London finally began to pay a little more attention to the Beatles. The British media coined the term, "Beatlemania." The Beatles began to perform at more prestigious venues, including the Royal Albert Hall in London. The Beatles were invited to appear on *Sunday Night at the London Palladium,* a nationally televised variety show watched by millions nationwide. The London Palladium was a very prestigious venue. After the performance, the fans outside mobbed the Beatles, who barely managed to get away. This had become a normal occurrence up north, but now it had spread to London. More major London newspapers took notice and reported the mania. One headline screamed, "Beatles Flee in Palladium TV Siege."

"Just rattle your jewelry"

The Beatles and Brian decided to move to London. Brian also moved his business operation there. After all, London was the entertainment capital and it also made it much easier to get to Abbey Road Studios. Shortly after the Palladium performance, they left for a short engagement in Sweden. They met with the Swedish media, taped a show for Swedish television, and performed in a few shows before returning to London.

Upon their arrival, they were surprised to find thousands of screaming fans waiting for them at London's Heathrow airport. The fans had brought the airport to a standstill. Coincidently, the British Prime Minister was at the airport to catch a flight out, but he had to wait until

"Operation Beatles" was complete. Apparently, the Ministry of Aviation had issued a directive giving the Beatles' arrival priority over the Prime Minister's departure. By chance, there was another important person at the airport that witnessed the frenzy that day. It was Ed Sullivan, the host of the *Ed Sullivan Show*, a popular national television variety show in America. When he saw the huge welcome for the Beatles, he decided to invite the Beatles to appear on his program.

The Beatles had been invited to perform for British royalty at the Royal Variety Show at the Prince of Wales Theatre in London. This was unlike anything they had done before because this audience consisted of members of the Royal family and other distinguished dignitaries. Like their other performances, fans gathered in large numbers outside the theatre, waiting and screaming. The Queen was pregnant and could not attend, but the Queen Mother and Princess Margaret did attend.

The Beatles were quite nervous, but performed admirably and even cracked a couple of amusing quips. At the end of their performance, John announced, "For our last number I'd like to your help. The people in the cheaper seats clap your hands and the rest of you just rattle your jewelry." That got quite a big laugh from everyone and applause, a big feat considering the conservative audience and it played right into the hands of the media. Every major newspaper had considerable coverage on the event. Beatlemania had now reached the upper echelons of British society and Britain had been conquered. Brian now set his sights on America and flew there immediately to make arrangements for their next conquest.

In late November, *With The Beatles* album was released and as expected, shot up to number one immediately. A week later, "I Want to Hold Your Hand/This Boy" single was released also topped the charts instantly.

The Beatles meet the Queen Mother at the Royal Variety Show.

They continued touring the country to packed theatres and screaming fans and kept up with their television and radio shows appearances. They even managed to put on a Christmas show for children. They wore costumes and did humorous skits. It was a nice change from the usual performances.

1963 was coming to an end. The year had started fairly quiet, but ended with a bang. There wasn't a soul in Britain that had not heard or seen them. They had exchanged their leather jackets and wild stage shows for suits, ties, and respectful bowing at the end of each show. They had lost their freedom to step outside without hindrance; yet, they managed to hold on to their seemingly radical hairstyles, sense of humor, and charming personalities that enthralled everyone who met them. The one question that was on everyone's mind was, "How soon

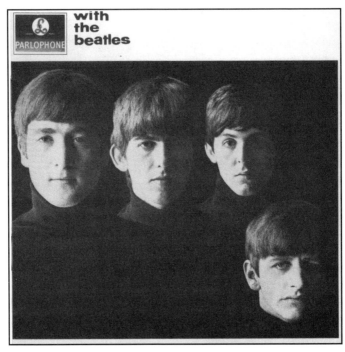

Above: Front cover of *With the Beatles*.

Below: *With the Beatles* song list.

with the beatles

[1] **IT WON'T BE LONG**
(Lennon/McCartney)

[2] **ALL I'VE GOT TO DO**
(Lennon/McCartney)

[3] **ALL MY LOVING**
(Lennon/McCartney)

[4] **DON'T BOTHER ME**
(Harrison)

[5] **LITTLE CHILD**
(Lennon/McCartney)

[6] **TILL THERE WAS YOU**
(Willson)

[7] **PLEASE MISTER POSTMAN**
(Dobbin-Garrett-Garman-Brianbert)

[8] **ROLL OVER BEETHOVEN**
(Berry)

[9] **HOLD ME TIGHT**
(Lennon/McCartney)

[10] **YOU REALLY GOT A HOLD ON ME**
(Robinson)

[11] **I WANNA BE YOUR MAN**
(Lennon/McCartney)

[12] **DEVIL IN HER HEART**
(Drapkin)

[13] **NOT A SECOND TIME**
(Lennon/McCartney)

[14] **MONEY**
(Bradford/Gordy)

℗ 1963 ORIGINAL SOUND RECORDINGS
MADE BY EMI RECORDS LTD.
© 1963 EMI RECORDS LTD

0 7777-46436-2 7

AAD
CDP 7 46436 2
(DIDX 1255)

will the bubble burst?" The answer depended upon whether American teenagers would succumb to Beatlemania. "I Want to Hold Your Hand" was scheduled for release in January. Would it face the same fate as their earlier singles in America that were largely ignored?

Beatle Bits

Some of the television variety shows the Beatles frequently appeared on in 1962 and 1963:

Thank Your Lucky Stars
Scene at 6:30
Ready Steady Go!
Juke Box Jury
People and Places
Tuesday Rendezvous
625 Special
The Morecambe and Wise Show

Above: Ringo holding a 'TLES' sign made by British European Airways (BEA) staff.

Below: John and Paul having fun over a newspaper article about Paul.

4

The American Dream

A New Frontier

When Brian was in America, he booked six major performances for the Beatles. There were three appearances scheduled on Ed Sullivan's popular television variety show, two performances at the world famous Carnegie Hall in New York City, and one performance at the Coliseum in Washington, D.C. Brian managed to accomplish this even though virtually no one had heard of the Beatles in America. Previous releases of their singles on Vee-Jay Records had not generated any interest. Finally, Capitol Records agreed to distribute and promote "I Want to Hold Your Hand" prior to the Beatles arrival in America.

"There is, undeniably, something about the United States which exceeds every other nation in practically every respect. We knew that America would make us or break us as world stars. In fact she made us."

Brian Espstein, Beatles manager.

Brian and the Beatles were quite apprehensive about their American trip. President Kennedy had just been assassinated and the country was in mourning. British artists had very limited success there previously. Elvis Presley and other American artists were dominant around the world, exercising tremendous influence on everyone, including the Beatles. The Beatles always viewed America with awe: a place they had read about, dreamed about, but never thought they might actually perform there.

Then there was simply the enormous size of the American market. It was several times the size of Britain's. American teenagers seemed to be on the cutting edge of everything. It seemed everything that Americans had or did was bigger, better or faster than the rest of the world. Brian wrote, "There is, undeniably, something about the United States which exceeds every other nation in practically every respect. We know that America would make us or break us as world stars. In fact, she made us."

Prior to the trip to America, the Beatles performed at the Olympia Theatre in Paris, France for three weeks in January. The reception by fans in Paris was fairly low key in comparison, but by the end of their trip, it became more frenzied. While in Paris, they recorded German versions of "She Loves You" and "I Want to Hold Your Hand" because they were advised that it was the only way to sell records in Germany. This turned out to be a false prediction.

"You are Number One in America!"

Meanwhile, in America, a disc jockey at a radio station in Washington, D.C. received a copy of "I Want to Hold Your Hand" from a friend and played it on the air before it was officially released. The radio station was inundated with inquiries about the song and requests poured in. Copies of the song made its way to several radio stations around the country and they experienced the same reaction. At the same time, there was an increase in coverage by the American media about Beatlemania in Britain. In addition to some national television news coverage, the Beatles appeared on the cover of some prestigious national American publications. Capitol Records recognized an opportunity and drastically increased the number of records they were going to produce for the upcoming release of "I Want To Hold Your Hand."

On January 13, 1964 "I Want to Hold Your Hand/I Saw Her Standing There" was released in America. The B side was different than the one released in England. Capitol Records also changed the selection on the Beatles LPs. They decided to release their own combination of songs on singles and albums that they felt was more suitable for the American market. Shortly after "I Want To Hold Your Hand," they released the album *Meet The Beatles* just for this market and it contained only twelve songs instead of the usual fourteen previously released in Britain. Also, this album had both sides of the single just released, which the Beatles wanted to avoid. In addition, the album was a combination of songs from albums previously released in Britain as well as some singles. These types of changes happened to their records around the world. The Beatles found out that they didn't have much control in these matters.

To complicate matters, Vee-Jay Records, which had released the earlier Beatles singles in America without much success, asserted its rights to some Beatles songs, releasing their own combination of songs in an album called *Introducing the Beatles*. For American fans, this was extraordinary; all of a sudden, they were flooded with several new Beatles songs.

A few days after the release of "I Want to Hold Your Hand," Brian told the Beatles, "You are Number One in

America!" "I Want to Hold Your Hand" had topped the charts instantaneously. Everyone was completely ecstatic. It was just unbelievable. Less than a month before, hardly anybody in America knew who the Beatles were. Now they were going there with a number one record in the country.

"The Beatles Are Coming!"

The Beatles got another big send off from their fans at Heathrow Airport in London as they departed for New York City on February 7, 1964, accompanied by a small contingent of reporters. They really didn't know what to expect from this trip. They were anxious, but excited. New York radio stations, especially a WINS disc jockey who went by "Murray the K," continuously hyped the arrival of the Beatles. Capitol Records promoted Beatles wigs and distributed posters and stickers with the slogan "The Beatles Are Coming." Newspaper and television reports added fuel to the anticipation. There were several thousand requests for tickets to see the Beatles on the *Ed Sullivan Show* in a studio that seated just a few hundred. All the performances at Carnegie Hall and Washington's Coliseum sold out quickly.

They landed at John F. Kennedy International Airport in New York to an estimated crowd of 5,000 screaming fans and a large contingent of reporters. They gave a press conference in which they won over the reporters with their charm and quick wit. Many of the questions asked were quite ridiculous, but the Beatles managed to respond with a touch of humor. The media seemed to be obsessed with the Beatles' hair. They were asked if they were bald under those 'wigs' and Ringo responded they were all bald. Another wondered if they would get a haircut at all and George replied, "I had one yesterday" resulting laughter around the room. Not everyone welcomed the Beatles with open arms. A small

Daily Mirror

Fans on a roof at London Airport wave goodbye to the Beatles yesterday.

3d.　Saturday, February 8, 1964　No. 18,704

YEAH! YEAH! U.S.A!

That old Beatlemania hits New York as a screaming girl tries to reach the Beatles.

Paul, Ringo, George and John answer questions at the Press conference.

IRENE GOES HOME TODAY

PRINCESS Irene of Holland, whose romance has started a constitutional crisis, is going home today.

This was announced in The Hague last night by the Dutch Government.

Retreat

The announcement added that Irene—who really became a Roman Catholic—had been spending several days in a "house of retreat" in Spain.

A second Government statement denied rumours that Queen Juliana might

'Some good news soon'

abdicate because of differences with the Cabinet over the romance.

Meanwhile Holland's Crown Princess Beatrix and her sister Margriet returned home yesterday from Austria, where they have been watching the winter Olympics.

Their father, Prince Bernhard, flew his own plane to Austria to collect them.

Meanwhile, in Madrid, Irene's secretary said that she "will soon be able to announce some good news in respect of her private life."

Overcome

It went on: "The princess has overcome the difficulties she had encountered in her spirit."

The statement denied that 24-year-old Irene's suitor was Prince Alfonso de Bourbon, grandson of the last King of Spain.

5,000 scream 'welcome' to the Beatles

From BARRIE HARDING
New York, Friday

FIVE thousand screaming, chanting teenagers—most of them playing truant from school—gave the Beatles a fantastic welcome here today.

More than 100 extra police were on duty to control the crowd as the group's jet landed at the John F. Kennedy Airport.

'Mad'

Pandemonium broke out among the stamping, banner-waving fans as the Beatles—John Lennon, Paul McCartney, George Harrison and Ringo Starr—stepped from the plane.

One policeman who has worked at the airport for ten years said: "I think the world has gone mad."

And a veteran airport employee said: "I see it—but I don't believe it."

Then, when the group had left the plane, thousands of their screaming fans rushed to the balcony above the Customs Hall to watch them pass through.

There were screams and shouts as their guitars appeared on a luggage trolley.

There were fresh squeals as the Beatles finally appeared, surrounded by a "bodyguard" of New York policemen.

Fans waved huge posters. There was a huge banner which proclaimed "Welcome to Beatlesville, U.S.A."

One of the fans had travelled 1,500 miles from Arkansas to see the group arrive—and many more had travelled up to 300 miles.

Airport officials said the crowd rivalled anything since General MacArthur returned from Korea.

The airport Press conference which followed the Beatles' arrival was chaos. Hundreds of reporters and photographers, plus seven T V cameras, had the room bursting at its seams. Part of the question-and-answer session between reporters and Beatles went like this:

"Will you sing something?"

John Lennon: "No!"

"Can you sing?"

"Not without money."

"How much money do you expect to make in the USA?"

George Harrison: "About half a crown."

"Are you going to get haircuts?"

Lennon: "We had one yesterday."

Hits

They were also asked what they thought of an anti-Beatle campaign in the mid-West, where some motorists were exhibiting stickers saying: "Stamp Out The Beatles."

Lennon replied: "We have a campaign to stamp out Detroit."

● The Beatles were told just before leaving London that their records "I Wanna Hold Your Hand" and "She Loves You" were joint No. 1 in the US Hit Parade group of boys in Detroit had protested with signs to "stamp out the Beatles." When asked for a comment on that, Paul replied that they were going to "stamp out Detroit!"

Even the normally reserved *New York Times* got in on the frenzy and headlined the arrival, "The Beatles Invade, Complete with Long Hair and Screaming Fans." That evening on the news, television stations coast to coast reported the arrival of the Beatles. The *Washington Post* wrote in an editorial, "After suffering the onslaught of American popular music for many years, the British are taking fiendish revenge. They have sent us the Beatles. This quartet of male singers has already been squashed and besieged by mobs of screeching teenagers in a demonstration that Elvis Presley must have contemplated with gloomy envy."

On the way to the hotel, the Beatles were amazed at the interest their arrival had generated as they listened to radio reports about them and about their drive to the hotel. One of the biggest differences between Britain and the United States at that time was the large number of radio and television stations available in every city in America.

Outside the elegant Plaza Hotel, where the Beatles were staying, hundreds of fans gathered. Security at the hotel was extremely tight. Many fans tried to con or sneak their way into the hotel, only to be caught and thrown out. Two girls placed themselves in a large package hoping to be delivered to the Beatles at the hotel, but were unsuccessful. The scene was something out of the ordinary, even for New Yorkers. Beatles songs were heard constantly on the radio, but the Beatles wanted to hear American songs. They called up several radio stations requesting songs they wanted to hear. In fact, they had a number of small radios tuned into different stations and when a song they liked came up, they would turn up the volume on that particular radio.

The Beatles pose with Ed Sullivan.

Beatle Bits

Songs performed by the Beatles on three Ed Sullivan *Shows:*

All My Loving	From Me to You
Till There Was You	Twist and Shout
She Loves You	Please Please Me
I Saw Her Standing There	She Loves You
I Want to Hold Your Hand	This Boy

In the Washington and New York concerts, they played all the songs on the Ed Sullivan Shows along with "Roll over Beethoven," "I Wanna Be Your Man," and "Long Tall Sally."

"Ladies and gentlemen, the Beatles"

The next morning they went to Central Park for a photo session, but George had to stay in bed because of a sore throat. They managed to enjoy themselves despite having a group of reporters and fans surround them. After another press conference and more interviews, they went to the Ed Sullivan Theatre for rehearsal without George. The next afternoon, they made their first appearance on the *Ed Sullivan show*, but the show was taped and was going to be aired after they returned to Britain. The *Ed Sullivan Show* was shown once a week on Sunday nights. The next appearance on the show was scheduled for 8 pm that evening and was going to be broadcast live around the country.

Prior to the broadcast, the Beatles received a telegram from Elvis wishing them success. Ed Sullivan read the telegram to the television audience. When Ed Sullivan introduced the Beatles on February 9, 1964 and said, "Ladies and gentlemen, the Beatles," television history was made in America. The broadcast broke all viewing records that held for several years as more than 73 million Americans -- teenagers and adults -- watched the show. It was reported that crime was almost non-existent during the ten minutes the Beatles were performing. They performed twice in the show. The opened the show, and after the other acts had their turn, they closed the show with another performance. During the first performance, the names of each of the Beatles appeared on the screen and when John's name appeared, they added, "Sorry, girls - he's married."

America had caught the bug. Beatlemania had officially spread there. Historians have noted this performance on the *Ed Sullivan Show* as a significant event in American pop culture because it broke a barrier that allowed numerous British groups to enter the gigantic American market. This was dubbed as "The British Invasion." Those who watched the show that night still have vivid memories of that historical moment. Fortunately, for the rest of us, all three shows are now available on digital videodisc (DVD).

A Capitol Welcome

The Beatles took the train to Washington, D.C. because their flight was canceled due to heavy snow. Despite the weather, thousands of fans greeted them at the train station. They performed in their first full concert in America on February 11, 1964, at the Washington Coliseum in front of another large, frenzied, jelly bean-throwing crowd similar to those in Britain. To make matters worse, the jellybeans in America were harder than their British counterparts. The *Washington Star* reported that an elderly police officer at the concert found the noise too loud and stuck a couple of bullets in his ears as plugs.

The stage was in the center of the venue with fans all around. To let all the fans see them, the Beatles moved to a different side of the stage every couple of songs. Ringo's drum kit was perched on a platform that was supposed to turn when the other guys moved, but it got stuck. So they had to turn his drums every time the sides changed!

The Beatles also attended a reception at the British Embassy in Washington. The Beatles were very annoyed at the behavior of some of the normally restrained dignitaries who aggressively sought autographs. In one incident, a guest clipped a lock of Ringo's hair, nearly cutting his ear. Gatherings like these were the most despised part of the Beatles' tour itinerary.

Sun, Sand, and Sea

They returned to New York for two shows at the prestigious Carnegie Hall. They continued having to deal with a throng of reporters and hundreds of hysterical fans. Fortunately, the next stop on their brief visit was to warm and sunny Florida where they hoped to get a break and rest for a while. They were greeted by dozens of reporters and thousands of fans at Miami airport and on the streets on their way to their hotel. The press coverage in Miami was very impressive. The second live *Ed Sullivan Show* was performed in a hall at the beachfront hotel they were staying at and also drew about seventy million viewers.

The Beatles got the chance to meet a very famous boxer, Cassius Clay, later known as Muhammad Ali. After a few fun-filled days in the sun, the Beatles returned to London to another tumultuous welcome from thousands of fans at the airport - a scene they had grown accustomed to seeing. They had just conquered America - something they couldn't even imagine in their wildest dreams.

A few weeks after they left, they broke another American record. On April 4, 1964, they had twelve songs on a top 100 music chart including the top five songs:

1. Can't Buy Me Love
2. Twist and Shout
3. I Want To Hold Your Hand
4. Do You Want To Know A Secret
5. Roll Over Beethoven

This feat has not been repeated or surpassed.

George opening some of the thousands of cards and gifts he received
from his fans for his twenty-first birthday.

5

Across the Universe

A Hard Day's Night

Shortly after they returned from America, they began shooting their first movie, *A Hard Day's Night*. In the autumn of 1963, just when Beatlemania caught on in Britain, Brian agreed to a movie deal featuring the Beatles. Since the plot hadn't been determined, the scriptwriter spent a few days with the Beatles. He saw how Beatlemania affected the lives of the Beatles and decided to make the movie reflecting a day in the life of the Beatles. He also experienced first hand their sense of humor and quick wit, which became an integral part of the movie. The writer also

The Beatles and some cast members on the special train used on *A Hard Day's Night.*

included a character that played Paul's wayward grandfather as an additional twist to the story.

The budget for the movie was quite low and was filmed in black and white. It also had to be completed in just a few weeks. Since none of the Beatles had acting experience, he kept their lines short and simple. Although they were quite nervous making the movie, they had a lot of fun. They tried to follow the script as best they could, but they would find themselves ad-libbing often and making everyone on the set laugh. However, most of the ad-libbing did not make it on to the film.

There was some debate about the title of the movie. Beatlemania was the working title. John suggested A *Hard Day's Night*. It was something Ringo had said previously. Ringo had a habit of misusing phrases. In this case, one day they had been working long hours and when they were finished, Ringo commented, "it's been a hard day" before realizing it was dark outside and completed his comment by adding "day's night."

The Beatles also had to complete the soundtrack for the movie. John and Paul had been writing and recording songs for the movie during the mania in Britain and America. When the title was set, the producer requested a song with the title in it. They wrote it that evening and played it back to the producer in the morning. This was just another example of their incredible talent. The album, with thirteen new songs, was the first one with all original compositions by the Beatles. The movie and the album were scheduled to premiere in July after the Beatles returned from their upcoming world tour.

Beatle Bits

George met his future wife, Pattie Boyd, on the movie set. Pattie, a professional model, played the part of a schoolgirl on the train used for the movie.

John added another mark of distinction to his creative work. His first book, *In His Own Write* was published in March 1964. It was a collection of short stories, jokes, poetry and drawings.

Above: Front cover of *A Hard Day's Night.*

Below: Back cover of *A Hard Day's Night*

```
 *[1] A Hard Day's Night
 *[2] I Should Have Known Better
 *[3] If I Fell
 *[4] I'm Happy Just to Dance With You
 *[5] And I Love Her
 *[6] Tell Me Why
 *[7] Can't Buy Me Love
 [8] Any Time at All
 [9] I'll Cry Instead
[10] Things We Said Today
[11] When I Get Home
[12] You Can't Do That
[13] I'll Be Back
```

℗ 1964 ORIGINAL SOUND RECORDINGS MADE BY
EMI RECORDS LTD.
© 1964 EMI RECORDS LTD.

* FROM THE SOUNDTRACK OF THE UNITED ARTISTS FILM
'A HARD DAY'S NIGHT'

WORDS AND MUSIC:
JOHN LENNON AND PAUL McCARTNEY

A Hard Day's Night song list.

Bon Voyage

The Beatles were preparing to leave for concerts in Denmark, the Netherlands and Hong Kong on route to a tour of Australia and New Zealand when Ringo was suddenly hospitalized with tonsillitis. They discussed whether they should cancel the tour. George was quite adamant about not touring until Ringo was ready. After much debate, they decided to go on with the tour with a substitute drummer since Ringo would likely be available in a few days. Jimmy Nicol, a professional drummer, was asked to join them and they managed to get in a few rehearsals with him before they left on the tour. Thousands gathered at the airport to wish them good-bye.

Fans in Denmark were just as wild as the rest of the places, bringing downtown Copenhagen to a standstill. In Amsterdam, the Beatles took a boat tour of the city in the city's canals. Thousands of fans lined the edges, some even diving into the water in an attempt to reach their boat, only to be stopped by the accompanying police patrol boats. The Beatles saw some people wearing capes that caught their eye. At one point in the boat tour, Mal, one of their road managers, swam to shore and bought a fan's cape.

In Hong Kong, fans were upset at not being able to get more than a glimpse of the Beatles at neither the airport nor outside the hotel because the police, numbering in the hundreds, surrounded the thousands of fans. The *Hong Kong Tiger Standard* headlined, "Police Zeal Spoils the Fans' Fun." The Beatles were disappointed that they weren't able to go sightseeing and shopping because the police couldn't ensure their safety. Hong Kong is a shopper's paradise, so arrangements were made to bring tailors, jewelers and other vendors to their hotel room. The Beatles bought quite bit of stuff and also had capes similar to the ones in Amsterdam tailor-made for them. They bought some presents for Ringo. They performed two shows, the first of which had the average screaming teenaged fan while the other had mostly British Army personnel who were quite reserved. Hong Kong was under British control at that time. At the press conference, they were asked what they thought of Chinese girls. Paul replied, "Those we've seen so far are great." After they left, souvenir hunters ransacked their hotel room.

Down Under

It was dark, cold, windy and rainy when the Beatles landed in Sydney, Australia. In spite of this, there were a couple of thousand fans waiting in the rain for them. The Beatles, wearing the capes just made in Hong Kong, stood on the back of an open, flat-bed truck, which paraded them around the airport so the fans could see them. They were completely drenched by the time they got to the hotel and,

The Beatles greet their fans from their hotel balcony.

to make matters worse, they were covered in blue from the dye in the capes!

As the Beatles toured Australia and New Zealand, they encountered some of the largest and most demonstrative crowds of fans ever gathered in the streets to see them. Police in various cities estimated that crowds of 100,000 to 300,000 lined the streets, sometimes comprising of more than half the population of those cities. The response by the people down under shouldn't have been a surprise since the Beatles songs had held the top six positions in the record charts before their arrival.

Security became a very big issue as some cities provided very little security and there were times when the Beatles were quite concerned about their safety. When Ringo arrived in Australia about half-way through the tour, thousands greeted him. The crowd around the hotel entrance was too thick to get Ringo inside the hotel safely. A police officer lifted Ringo onto his shoulders and tried to make a run into the hotel. Unfortunately, he tripped and Ringo landed in the crowd. Fortunately, the officer managed to free Ringo and got him inside the hotel safely. They weren't able to leave the security of their hotel rooms except for dozens of official functions, which the Beatles despised and tried to avoid whenever possible. When some dignitaries weren't able to get easy access to the Beatles, they complained to the local press. The press, however, provided mostly positive coverage of the Beatles.

The throwing of jelly babies towards the stage, which had become a common sight everywhere, had become unmanageable in Australia and New Zealand. The Beatles even stopped some concerts and asked the fans to stop, but were only met with shrieks and more jelly babies. Even miniature stuffed koala bears and gift wrapped packages were thrown. While John, Paul, and George managed to get out of the way most of the time, poor Ringo, seated at the drums, had to endure the pelting. They knew that this was simply a way of showing affection and tried to put up with it, but were getting fed up.

In Brisbane, the last stop on the tour, they encountered some trouble at the airport. While they were being paraded on an open bed truck around the airport upon their arrival, some envious protesters threw eggs and tomatoes at them. Despite all they had to put up with, the Beatles managed to enjoy their tour of Australia and New Zealand, although they never returned there together again.

Beatle Bits

John's aunt Mimi traveled to Australia and New Zealand with the Beatles to visit relatives.

No Place like Home

A Hard Day's Night premiered at the London Pavilion on July 6, 1964. The Beatles, as well as some members of the Royal family, were in attendance. Due to the large crowds gathered around the theatre, roads around the Pavilion had to be completely shut down to traffic. The Beatles felt a bit embarrassed watching themselves on the big screen as they always felt they could have done even better. They knew it only portrayed one aspect of their lives, but were quite happy with the results.

The movie was a critical and commercial success around the world. Now teenagers in the far reaches of the world could experience Beatlemania. It was reported that many teenagers went to see the movie numerous times during its run. In many cases, the scene in many theatres was similar to their concerts - continuous screaming from fans. The album and the title track, "A Hard Day's Night" were released and quickly topped the charts.

A few days later, the Beatles went to Liverpool for the movie's premiere there. An estimated one hundred thousand fans welcomed them home. They were quite surprised at the greeting from their hometown. They had heard that many people there weren't happy that the Beatles had left Liverpool and thought that the Beatles had forgotten them. The Beatles felt quite strange waving to the people who lined the very same streets they used to walk down just a couple of years ago without being noticed. These were the same streets they grew up playing and shopping on.

A civic reception was held in their honor with many of their childhood friends and family in attendance. It was, without a doubt, their finest hour.

Daily Mirror

SAT. JULY 11 1964

© The Daily Mirror Newspapers, Ltd., 1964

Telephone: FLEet-street 0246

They're back—and it's the biggest thing that has ever hit Liverpool

100,000 ROAR
THE BEATLES HOME

Brambell ... as Steptoe.

'I LOST MY PADDY' SAYS STEPTOE

ACTOR Wilfrid "Steptoe" Brambell walked out of a welcome for the Beatles last night.

He said: "The least that Liverpool officials might have done was to learn just the 'A' of the 'ABC' of manners."

Instead of going to the Liverpool premiere of the film "A Hard Day's Night," in which he plays Paul McCartney's grandfather, he left for London.

At his hotel he said: "As soon as I got inside the town hall, an ignorant policeman said: 'You can't sign autographs here. This is the Beatles' party, not yours.'

"He said he was pushed by the police.

Irish-born Mr. Brambell added: "I have an Irish paddy, but I don't often lose my temper. I lost it tonight."

Street of stretcher cases.... This was the scene during yesterday's fantastic Beatles welcome.

ONE hundred thousand frenzied fans welcomed the Beatles home to Liverpool yesterday.

"This is the biggest thing that's ever happened here," said Liverpool's Chief Constable.

And the group's manager, Brian Epstein, added: "This is the greatest welcome we have ever had ANYWHERE in the world. It is fantastic, fabulous, and unbelievable."

At least forty people caught in the crush were taken to hospital.

One hospital had to close its casualty ward because it could take no more cases.

400 fans injured

Swaying

Ambulance men treated more than 400 who fainted in the swaying, screaming crowds.

It all started at 5.28 p.m. when the Beatles' airliner touched down at Speke airport, Liverpool.

•Five thousand screaming banner-waving fans were waiting.

But all that most of them saw of their idols were the mopheads submerged in a sea of policemen.

All police leave in the city had been suspended—and reinforcements were rushed to the airport in double-decker buses.

Chief Constable Smith was brushed aside as the fans broke through a cordon and tried to touch the Beatles.

And the storming welcome went on all the way along the seven-mile route to the town hall.

reception at the town hall the Beatles came across the Liverpool City Police Band.

Paul McCartney grabbed a trumpet, George Harrison a horn, and Ringo whipped the conductor's baton from the hands of a chief inspector.

•HOBSEY NOTE . . . Drakes Drum, the racehorse bought by Beatle Paul for his father looks a sound each-way bet today, writes Newsboy. See Page 20.

Linked

As the Beatles' limousine, followed by two official cars, crawled into the centre of the city the police linked arms and leaned at an angle of forty-five degrees to keep back the cheering crowds.

Castle-street, in front of the town hall, was jammed with people—and three mobile first aid stations worked at top pressure.

When the Beatles appeared on the balcony of the town hall with the Lord Mayor, Alderman Louis Caplan, the crowd went crazy.

Casualties rose from their stretchers on the pavement and fought men and women police to get back in front of the town hall.

On their way to the reception at the town hall.

RHODESIA: PEACE TALK BID

By GORDON JEFFERY

BRITAIN is considering calling face-to-face "peace" talks on trouble-torn Southern Rhodesia.

The meeting would be between the country's African nationalist leaders and the white settler government of Premier Ian Smith.

Britain agreed to examine the possibility of a round-table settlement in the face of "action now" demands by African delegates at yesterday's session of the Commonwealth

Prime Ministers' Conference in London.

Commonwealth Secretary Duncan Sandys is expected to make an announcement when the Premiers resume their talks on Monday.

Kenya's Jomo Kenyatta opened the attack on British's attitude to Southern Rhodesia by demanding political equality for the

country's 3,500,000 Africans with the 221,000 whites.

He called for the release of African political prisoners and asked Britain to call a conference to fix a new constitution, based on "one man, one vote."

Both Mr. Kenyatta and President Julius Nyerere of Tanganyika are understood to have offered "military

aid" if Mr. Smith refused to start talks.

They made the offer after Mr. Sandys warned that there was little likelihood of the Smith Government agreeing to a conference.

Mr. Sandys also warned that attempts to pressurise the Southern Rhodesian Government might provoke Mr. Smith to carry out his threat to declare the country independent.

Pledge

He pledged that Britain would not recognise a unilateral declaration and would not grant independence unless the present constitution was amended.

But he admitted that some action was necessary to end the present "negative" position.

Mr. Kenyatta said he was not convinced by the argument that Britain had no control over Southern Rhodesian affairs.

He called for an end to British "vagueness" over the issue.

Makarios gets big guns

From DONALD WISE

Nicosia, Friday

THE Greek-Cypriot army admitted today that it has imported heavy artillery to the island

ARIAS IMPROVING

Dame Margot Fonteyn's husband, Dr. Roberto Arias, critically ill at Stoke Mandeville Hospital, Bucks, showed some improvement last night.

Archbishop Makarios's army warned UN officers that it has ten 25-pounders shipped in from Egypt and would begin test-firing later today.

But UN observers say air-reconnaissance crews report at least twenty-five heavy guns massed in a park south-east of Nicosia.

And the crews are believed to be by Greek soldiers who have slipped on to the island through the port of Limassol, also thought to

be the route used for shipping the guns in.

Western Embassies suspect that there are now 5,000 Greek troops on the island, and that Turkish irregulars are landing nightly on the Turkish-Cypriot sector in the north-west.

Last night Greek-Cypriots flung a security ring round Limassol, barring UN troops and Turkish-Cypriots. Then large convoys of covered lorries headed inland.

FOUR TRAPPED IN CRASH CARS

FOUR people were trapped when two cars collided in the road near Datchet, Bucks, last night. They were freed by firemen and taken to hospital.

A Fire Brigade spokesman said: "All four people were injured." Traffic was held up while breakdown trucks were called from nearby garages.

For straight pineapple juice, drink a BRITVIC

Britvic is the name for pure, undiluted fruit juices bottled straight from the fresh fruit.

You can't beat the real thing!

Printed and Published by THE DAILY MIRROR NEWSPAPERS Ltd., at Holborn Circus, London, E.C.1, and at Mark-lane, Manchester 4, Saturday, July 11, 1964.

Beyond the American Frontier

Their schedule continued at a hectic pace as they recorded more songs and performed at various venues around Britain, including a charity event at the Palladium, all the while keeping up with their television and radio appearances. With little time to rest, they left for a grueling month long, twenty-four city tour of the United States and Canada.

The Beatles arrived in San Francisco to another huge crowd at the airport. At the customary press conference, Ringo was asked about his marriage plans. He joked that there were rumors that he was getting married every week, but he never would. The concert at the Cow Palace had the usual continuous screams from hysterical fans with the noise reaching jet engine levels while the police barely managed to keep fans off the stage. Several fans required first aid treatment. The *San Francisco Chronicle* called it the "Wildest Night at Cow Palace." The media and some fans criticized the short performance. The average performance lasted from about twenty to thirty minutes.

As the Beatles traveled from city to city, this scenario was repeated throughout the tour. Reporters at press conferences in different cities asked the same questions asked over and over again. It appeared that the press was obsessed with the amount the Beatles were earning on this tour. Hysterical fans, occasionally unmanageable and unruly, continued to confine the Beatles to their rooms. On rare occasions, the Beatles managed to sneak into town for a brief period, usually very late at night with the help of some friendly police officers. Politicians, local celebrities, and even the police irritated the Beatles by asking for preferential treatment and autographs. The Beatles were also unhappy with the extremely tight security

Police surround the stage to protect the Beatles (above),
but a girl still manages to elude them and grab a hold of George (below)

arrangements that barred their fans from getting a glimpse of the Beatles at many airports and hotels.

In Seattle, an ambulance had to be used as a ruse to transport the Beatles after the concert because fans had blocked the exits, which trapped the Beatles in their dressing room for nearly an hour. More than thirty-five fans needed first aid. In one case reported by the *Seattle Times*, a police officer aiding a female fan that had fainted during the concert asked her name. "Paul," she replied as she "swooned back into unconsciousness." The paper pointed out, for the sake of its adult readers, that Paul was one of the Beatles.

Thousands of fans without tickets who had gathered outside Vancouver's Empire Stadium scuffled with police as they tried to smash down an entry gate without success. After the concert, the Beatles dashed off the stage avoiding a surge of fans who stormed the stage and tore it apart for souvenirs. As the Beatles' motorcade left the stadium, someone threw a bicycle in front of the lead car in hopes of stopping them, but the motorcade managed to avoid the bicycle and continue without delay.

Live at the Hollywood Bowl

Performing at the famous Hollywood Bowl in Los Angeles was very exciting for the Beatles because they had always admired the venue. George Martin arranged for the concert to be recorded for an album because he knew they were a very good live band and wanted it captured on tape. The screams from the fans made it difficult to hear the songs. The project was shelved until 1977 when *The Beatles at the Hollywood Bowl* was released. At the press conference, they were asked their opinion about a report by psychiatrists that the Beatles were a menace. George responded, "Psychiatrists are a menace, too." They met several Hollywood celebrities at a private reception.

The *Denver Post* wrote, "The Browne Palace Hotel has hosted presidents, kings, queens, and movie stars, but there has never been a scene like Wednesday afternoon." When asked in Cincinnati what they'd do "when the wave of Beatlemania subsides," John responded sarcastically, "Count the money." Another reporter wanted to know what excuse they had for their long hair, John replied, "Well, it just grows out of our head." The *Cincinnati Enquirer* reported, "A technician from a television station was trying to measure the sound with an instrument. He gave up when the instrument recorded its maximum reading and broke."

The Beatles returned to New York for the first time since their visit in February. Despite arriving at 3 am, there were 3,000 fans waiting for them. The *New York Times* blamed the Beatles for the fans behavior. The paper wrote, "They have created a monster in their audience." In Atlantic City, they had to sneak out of their hotel in the back of a seafood delivery truck. At a press conference in Philadelphia, a reporter asked if they'd ever get a haircut. Ringo responded, "We might get bald."

A Day at the Races

In Indianapolis, they were asked what would happen if fans broke through the police barriers. One of the Beatles responded, "Die laughing." The reporter was unable to identify the Beatle in the *Indianapolis Star* article. The newspaper editor inserted, "(Our man couldn't tell them apart.)" The paper also reported that a sleepless Ringo got a tour of the city at dawn, escorted by state policemen. The Speedway Motel reported receiving 40,000 to 50,000 phone calls during the Beatles two day stay there. Before they departed, they were taken for a ride around the famous racetrack. George loved it and perhaps this may have been what sparked his interest in car racing many years later.

The Milwaukee Journal asked some teenagers to write about why they liked the Beatles. One teenager wrote, "These guys make you forget about the daily worldly problems." Another described herself as feeling "eternal for one moment, like a lake at dawn." The article added a father's point of view, presumably telling his daughter, "If I hear the word 'Beatle' once more after Friday night, I'll wring your neck." The father walked out whistling "A Hard Day's Night." A couple of boys carrying signs at the airport which read, "Beatles Go Home" and "Ringo's Sick" were charged by an angry mob of teenaged girls and the boys quickly fled without their signs.

More than 300 policemen were on hand at their concert in Chicago, backed up by 150 firemen and 200 ushers. The *Chicago Tribune* quoted a mother who said she felt sorry for the Beatles: "What will happen to them when all this adulation has passed them by?" In Detroit, a smiling Paul posed for a photo wearing a "To HELL with the BEATLES" button, which was a campaign started by students at the University of Detroit, according the *Detroit Daily Press.*

"34,000 Beatle Fans Pay $100,000 to Hear Themselves" was the headline in the *Toronto Star.* "A Beatle, for those over 18," the paper wrote, "is a young man with a shaggy hair-do just seven-eighths of inch shorter than mom's when she was a flapper, a musical talent and a stock of smart answers to foolish questions." The paper added that the weekend began like any other, "but before it ended, it became one of the most awesome weekends in the city's history." A police paddy wagon was used as a ruse to get the Beatles into and out of Maple Leaf Gardens unnoticed while police escorted empty limousines, which were used to create a diversion.

Beatle Bits

A Very Sick Fan Gets a VIP Phone Call

The Milwaukee Journal found out about a very sick fourteen-year-old Beatles fan who had been hospitalized for two weeks for an undetermined illness and was undergoing tests. The girl had a ticket to the Beatles concert, but was unable to go. The paper arranged for Paul to give the girl a surprise phone call at the hospital. The girl was quite shocked to hear from Paul, as one would expect. They had a brief, but pleasant chat according to the reporter who thought the girl was going to cry. "She wanted to," the reporter said, "if that room hadn't been full (of nurses), she would have." He added, "She said she wanted to take the telephone home with her. And then the nurses cried."

Hurricane Dora

The Beatles concert in Jacksonville was postponed as Hurricane Dora pounded the Jacksonville area with strong winds and heavy rains. Despite widespread damage, flooding, and power outages, over 20,000 showed up to see the Beatles perform at the rescheduled concert, just two days after the storm. *The Florida Times-Union* reported "Though Dora was far gone, the winds in the park blew Beatles hair in all directions and, at times, threatened the instruments."

"A Deafening Silence"

A death threat against Ringo in Montreal resulted in a plain-clothes police officer sitting near Ringo during the concert. "After Screaming, Fainting, Hysteria - A Deafening Silence" was the headline in the *Montreal Star* commenting on the departure of the Beatles from Montreal. The paper added, "The plane left for the relative peace and quiet of a Florida hurricane," referring to the impending hurricane approaching Jacksonville, the next stop in the Beatles itinerary. Due to Hurricane Dora, the Beatles' plane was diverted to Key West, Florida for one day before heading up to Jacksonville. Earlier, the Beatles had announced that they were not going to perform in Jacksonville if the fans were segregated because of color. There was no separate seating at the concert. Responding to yet another question about money at the press conference, John said, "We each got $140 when we arrived on tour and we've still got it. We have no place to spend money."

"An Astonishing Human Storm" read the headline in the *Boston Globe* after the concert. A teenaged girl told reporters she was upset that the fans were screaming all the time. "That's stupid," she complained, "I only scream when they're singing." Sixty to seventy screaming girls chased an eighteen-year old boy, wearing a Beatles haircut. He managed to escape only after the girls ripped off his shirt. "Beatles' arrival is like a Presidential Motorcade." said the *Pittsburgh Post-Gazette*, adding that "the security arrangements were equally or more elaborate than those for Presidential visits."

Police in Cleveland forcibly stopped the concert at the Public Hall for several minutes because they felt the fans were on the verge of storming the stage. The Beatles, having seen similar hysteria elsewhere, continued playing even though the police went on stage and asked them to stop. They stopped only after an officer took George by his arm and steered him forcefully backstage. The Beatles weren't pleased at the interruption, but Brian agreed with the police. The concert resumed after the crowd settled down to the satisfaction of the police.

A much-needed day off was taken up by a last minute concert addition to the schedule. A wealthy Kansas City owner of the local major league baseball team offered enough money to convince Brian to have the Beatles perform there. The Beatles weren't concerned about the money; they just wanted a day off, but Brian persuaded them to perform. Even at this early stage in their career, a *Kansas City Times* reporter noted that John and Paul "have been staking out a very respectable claim as one of the best song-writing teams in the business."

The Beatles were outfitted Texas-style - with ten-gallon hats - when they arrived in Dallas. The *Dallas Morning News* ran a story about a thirteen-year old girl who couldn't get into the hotel where the Beatles were staying despite having legitimate room reservations. The matter was resolved after her mother contacted the hotel. Unfortunately, the girl had lost her concert tickets, but she wasn't worried at that time. "Don't you know who's sleeping upstairs right now?" she asked the reporter. "That's the Beatles."

On their way to New York, their final stop on the tour, the Beatles took an unscheduled detour to Missouri. The owner of the chartered plane they were using invited them to spend a day at his ranch. They spent some time relaxing and riding horses. The concert in New York was for the benefit of United Cerebral Fund of New York. At their hotel, the Delmonico, they met Bob Dylan, an American folk legend they admired and frequently listened to. They returned to London to another rousing welcome at the airport.

Eight Days a Week

The Beatles barely had a chance to rest before beginning a month-long tour of Britain. As expected, the fan frenzy continued throughout the tour. They also got to perform in Belfast, Northern Ireland. Unlike the American tour, traveling wasn't a big issue because of the shorter distances between venues. Crowd control was also easier as most of these venues were much smaller than those in the United States. While they were on the tour, they also managed to return to London and complete recording their next album, *Beatles For Sale*. It was released in December and topped the charts taking out their own *A Hard Day's Night*. The American version of this LP, *Beatles '65* was released with a slightly different song list and quickly beat out Elvis' album for the top spot. They always seemed to find the time to record a number of singles and also continued to meet their obligations for their radio and TV shows appearances.

They took short separate vacations before beginning a three-week stint on *"Another Beatles' Christmas Show"* at the Hammersmith Odeon in London complete with skits and songs by the Beatles and other artists. Among the other artists in this show were the Yardbirds. Eric Clapton was a member who became one of George's best friends.

1964 turned out to be a whirlwind year for the Beatles. Starting with conquering America - an unimaginable feat - to the frenzied Australian tour to the rousing welcome home in Liverpool, it was a script that even Hollywood couldn't have conjured up. It's hard to imagine that in such a busy year, they also made a critically acclaimed and commercially successful movie as well as chart-topping albums and singles. They were truly working "Eight Days a Week."

Above: Front cover of *Beatles For Sale*.

Below: Back cover of *Beatles For Sale*.

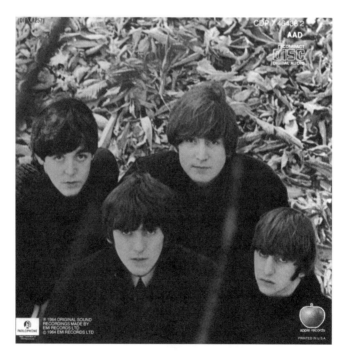

1	**NO REPLY**
	(Lennon/McCartney)
2	**I'M A LOSER**
	(Lennon/McCartney)
3	**BABY'S IN BLACK**
	(Lennon/McCartney)
4	**ROCK AND ROLL MUSIC**
	(Berry)
5	**I'LL FOLLOW THE SUN**
	(Lennon/McCartney)
6	**MR. MOONLIGHT**
	(Johnson)
7	**MEDLEY**
	a. KANSAS CITY
	(Lieber/Stoller)
	b. HEY, HEY, HEY, HEY
	(Penniman)
8	**EIGHT DAYS A WEEK**
	(Lennon/McCartney)
9	**WORDS OF LOVE**
	(Holly)
10	**HONEY DON'T**
	(Perkins)
11	**EVERY LITTLE THING**
	(Lennon/McCartney)
12	**I DON'T WANT TO SPOIL THE PARTY**
	(Lennon/McCartney)
13	**WHAT YOU'RE DOING**
	(Lennon/McCartney)
14	**EVERYBODY'S TRYING TO BE MY BABY**
	(Perkins)

℗ 1964 ORIGINAL SOUND RECORDINGS MADE
BY EMI RECORDS LTD
© 1964 EMI RECORDS LTD.

Beatles For Sale song list.

Ringo Starr with his new bride, Maureen.

6

Ticket to Ride

HELP!

In February 1965, Ringo married Maureen Cox whom he had met a few years back at the Cavern Club. After a brief honeymoon, he joined the rest of the Beatles as they headed to the Bahamas to start shooting their second film, *Help!* Unlike *A Hard Day's Night,* this movie was in color with both a plot and a fairly big budget. It was a zany, quirky, satirical musical comedy in which Ringo is sought by both, an Indian religious cult and mad scientists, all trying to recover a sacrificial ring worn by him while the other Beatles try to help him elude them.

Scene from *Help!*

The pursuit took them to the exotic beaches of the Bahamas, the mountains of Austria and then back to Britain. Although the scenes in the Bahamas were shot first, they would appear in the film after the scenes in Austria, so the Beatles had to be careful not to get a tan. The weather turned out to be quite cool, but they had to wear tropical clothing and act as if they were warm. They also tried their hand at skiing on the slopes of the Alps. It was George and Ringo's first attempt at skiing.

Although the Beatles were not thrilled with the plot, they had a lot of fun making the film and tested the patience of the crew. Many scenes had to be repeated several times because the Beatles would burst into hysterical fits of laughter. They felt that the best bits of the film never made it on to the film. They had a lot less control over their performance in *Help!* than they did in *A Hard Day's Night,* but the supporting cast of professional actors and actresses performed admirably.

The movie received mixed reviews from the critics, but was commercially successful around the world. It was a daunting task to try and improve on the critical success of *A Hard Day's Night*. The movie premiered in July at the London Pavilion with Princess Margaret in attendance. The scene outside the pavilion was similar to the opening of *A Hard Day's Night"* with thousands of fans gathering outside hoping for a glimpse of the Beatles.

Scrambled Eggs

Eight Arms to Hold You was the working title for *Help!* until near the end of the filming. It's not clear how the title *Help!* came about, but it seemed suitable for the story line. The producer asked John and Paul to come up with a title track just like he did for *A Hard Day's Night*. Once again, they wrote the song Help! in one evening and presented it to the producer the following morning. Although "Help!" was a collaborative effort, John wrote most of the lyrics. Many years later, John said that he was quite depressed at that time he wrote the song. It became his second introspective song after "I'm a Loser" which was recorded for *Beatles For Sale.*

They continued to work on several other songs for the movie soundtrack and it seems that they were always progressing with their techniques and sound. "You've Got to Hide Your Love Away" was the first major acoustic guitar recording for them. Ringo played the tambourine while professional session players were brought in to play the flute. "Ticket to Ride" had a harder edge and offered a fairly new sound. It was released as a single and topped the charts. Two of George's songs appeared on the album and revealed his improved development in songwriting.

Above: Front cover of *Help!*

Below: *Help!* song list.

Beatle Bits

Two incidents during the filming of *Help!* had a significant impact on the Beatles and especially affected George:

In the Bahamas, the Beatles were sitting on bicycles on the side of a road waiting for a scene to be filmed when an Indian man walked up to George and gave him a book on yoga. The man was from a town called Rishikesh in India. This began George's interest in Indian philosophy.

In London, they were filming a scene at an Indian restaurant and there was a group of Indian musicians playing in the background. George became very interested in their musical instruments, especially the sitar. Later, George learned to play the sitar and the Beatles became the first English language artists to record songs with Indian instruments.

Probably the most significant development at this time had to do with the song "Yesterday." Paul woke up one morning with a tune in his head and thought it might be an old jazz melody he might have heard previously, but he wasn't sure. He immediately played it in on his piano and asked several friends if they had heard it. When no one had, he began to write the words to it calling the song "Scrambled Eggs." He also used the words "scrambled eggs" in the song before he changed them to "yesterday."

After discussing the song with George Martin, it appeared that there wasn't much need for the others, so it was decided that only Paul would perform in the song. It marked the first time that a song had been recorded with only one Beatle singing and playing. Paul recorded "Yesterday" playing an acoustic guitar. Later George Martin added a professional string quartet for background music.

The Beatles did not want to release the song as a single in Britain because they felt such a ballad might be bad for their rock and roll image, but it was included on the *Help!* album. The song was released as a single in America and went to number one. "Yesterday" holds the record of being the most recorded song in history; an estimated 3,000 artists have covered the song. In addition, it also holds the record for being the most played song on American radio.

MBE

Queen Elizabeth II of England awarded John, Paul, George and Ringo the 'Member of the Most Excellent Order of the British Empire (MBE)' medal for their services to the country. The MBE is awarded annually to select individuals recommended by the Prime Minister for their contribution to British society in a variety of fields, and was typically given to government employees, military personnel, and aristocrats.

So it was not surprising that shortly after the announcement, many medal holders were in an uproar over awarding such an honor to the Beatles. Several returned their medals because they felt having the Beatles as MBEs had "debased and cheapened" it as an honor. However, there were many, young and old, who felt that the Beatles deserved the honor as they had significantly contributed to the British economy and were responsible for bringing in a lot of money from their foreign sales of the records, as well as from concert revenues. The press contributed to this uproar by giving this story massive coverage. The Beatles took it all in stride.

When the Beatles arrived at Buckingham Palace to accept the award, they were met by hordes of fans, many of which tried unsuccessfully to climb over the tall gates to get inside. When the Beatles met the Queen, they joked with

Daily Mirror

Now they are in the topmost chart of all

James Paul McCartney, Esq., MBE.   John Winston Lennon, Esq., MBE.   Richard (Ringo) Starkey, Esq., MBE.   ...and George Harrison, Esq., MBE.

4d.   Saturday, June 12, 1965   ✦ ✦ ✦   No. 19,120

BEATLES, MBE!

By DON SHORT

OH, what a surprise! The Beatles zoom into the topmost chart of all this morning — the Queen's Birthday Honours.

All four of the lads from Liverpool are made Members of the Order of the British Empire (MBE) in the Queen's first "pop" Honours list.

It's not a "pop" list just in terms of music but of popular entertainment. For honours also go to actress Violet Carson (Ena Sharples of "Coronation Street"); actor Jack Warner ("Dixon of Dock Green") and singer Frankie Vaughan.

It's a list that throws overboard, in a way, the

tradition of honours for conventional public service . . . and it will certainly run into stiff criticism by the diehards.

So the Birthday Honours list of 1965, featuring such non-traditionalists as the Beatles, will almost certainly be the most controversial ever issued. The Beatles now become ordi-

nary members of The Most Excellent Order of the British Empire and, unlike others honoured in the list, they have no other citation than that they are "Members of 'The Beatles.'"

Listed

They are listed as George Harrison, Esq., John Winston Lennon, Esq., James Paul Mc-Cartney, Esq., and Ringo Starr,

The big surprise in the Queen's first 'pop' Honours list

Esq. (Richard Starkey, Esq.).

They were unknown three years ago. Now their honour places them 120th in the 125 titles of precedence set out by Debrett's — the book which is the authority on saying who comes where in the social set-up.

Their MBEs give them precedence over younger sons of baronets and knights, Esquires and Gentlemen of Coat Armour.

Unknown three years ago . . . then, from the Cavern Cellar Club, Liverpool, they brought their new beat music to capture the top prizes of the pop music industry and the hearts of teenagers all over the world.

The mop-topped quartet are now something of a national possession

John, 25, son of a Liverpool hotel worker and born in the blitz; Paul, 22, steady friend of actress Jane Asher; George, 23, son of a corporation bus driver; and Ringo, messenger boy, ship's waiter and would-be hairdresser . . .

Twinkle

Maybe they were recommended for their honour by Mr. Harold Wilson with a twinkle in his eye.

For he was "bowled over" by them when he presented them with their Variety Club of Great Britain awards.

And maybe the Queen smiled, too, when she found their names on the list . . . and put her official seal on the decision to award them MBEs.

Rest of the Honours—See Page 4.

This is the MBE.

HOW DID THE LADS EARN THIS GONG?

By EDWARD VALE

WHY do the Beatles get the M.B.E.?

A spokesman at the Prime Minister's office, where the Honours List recommendations are drawn up, said: "We have to say, and we don't always say."

But a source close to Premier Harold Wilson said: "Well, the Beatles are leaders in their particular art."

But others will say that they deserve the honours as "exporters . . . for they have earned millions of dollars for Britain by their world-selling discs and personal appearances.

Medal

WHAT will they get? A silver medal, together with a pink ribbon edged with white. The ribbon can be sewn to a clasp and pinned to the left breast.

HOW will they get their awards? They will be invited to Buckingham Palace, where the Queen or another member of the Royal Family will present them.

The date for their investiture has yet to be decided.

MBE? You're Joking of Course — See Donald Zec, Page 9.

her. When she asked how long had they had been together, Paul and Ringo answered in unison, "Forty years." They said the Queen had a "quizzical" look on her face.

In an interview many years later, John said, "Lots of people who complained about us receiving the MBE received theirs for heroism in war, for killing people. We received ours for entertaining other people. I'd say we deserve ours more." In 1969, John returned his medal to protest the British government's role in the Nigeria/Biafra conflict and its support of America in the Vietnam War.

The Matador

In June, the Beatles left on a two-week tour of France, Italy, and Spain. The level of enthusiasm varied from fairly subdued to hysteria. Some of the venues were half-full, especially during the afternoon shows; perhaps this was because the schools were in session. They still had to deal with frenzied fans and were concerned over the harsh manner with which the police handled some of the over-zealous fans. One memorable venue was the Plaza de Toros Las Ventas, in Madrid, a bullfighting arena. Some of the Beatles' entourage watched a bull fight there the day before the concert. Ringo found it to be quite distressing.

Then they left for a three-week, ten-city tour of United States and Canada in August. It was considerably shorter than their previous year's tour. Before their arrival, the *New York Times* wrote, "In less than two years, the Beatles have inspired an upheaval in pop music, mores, fashion, hair styles and manners. They have helped conquer a number of adults with their charm, irreverent wit and musical skill. They have provided marching songs for the teen-age revolution." The paper also commented on the possibility of a slight decline of the Beatles' popularity, citing the recent European tour, as well as the increased competition from many new British and American artists. Their 1964 tour set the bar quite high.

Play Ball

When their plane landed at New York's Kennedy Airport, they saw a large crowd of fans gathered at the terminal to greet them. To the dismay of the Beatles and the fans, however, the plane stopped quite a distance away from the terminal for security reasons and whisked the Beatles to the Warwick hotel in the awaiting limousine. Thousands of fans had surrounded their hotel, but were not able to see the Beatles because of tight security. They had booked an entire floor for their entourage. At the press conference, the Beatles complained about the fans being unable to see them at the airport. Several celebrities, including Bob Dylan, visited the Beatles that night.

The following day they recorded a performance for the *Ed Sullivan Show* to be broadcast after the end of the tour. Paul sang "Yesterday" for the first time in front of a live audience. It seemed that every time they reached a milestone, there was another one waiting for them ahead. The year before, it was the *Ed Sullivan Show*. In 1965, it was Shea Stadium, home of the New York Mets baseball team where they played in front of more than 55,000 fans, the largest crowd ever assembled for a concert at that time.

Despite all the Beatles had experienced in the past two years, they were quite anxious about performing in front of such a large crowd. Due to security concerns, the Beatles were taken to a heliport near their hotel. They were then taken by helicopter to the top of the Pan Am building near the stadium. On their way, they flew over the stadium and got a view of the enormous crowd. Upon landing, they were driven in a Wells Fargo armored truck, complete with armed guards, to the stadium. Security at the stadium was very tight. There were an estimated 600 policemen on guard. Fences eight feet high were placed on the perimeter of the field to prevent fans from getting near the stage.

The Beatles' anxiety quickly faded away as soon as they got on stage, which was located on second base. They waved to the hysterical, screaming crowd and began playing. The Beatles enjoyed every minute of the concert. During the final song of the concert, "I'm Down," John was playing the organ and frequently used his elbow to play. They were all laughing during the song. Like most of their concerts, the crowd noise was earsplitting. "Shrieks of

The Beatles perform at Shea Stadium, New York, in front of a record-breaking crowd.

55,000 Accompany Beatles" was the headline in the *New York Times*. Another headline read "The Sky Glows over Queens as the Beatles Take Over Shea Stadium." It was another milestone in their astonishing journey.

About 300 girls required first aid after they fainted during the performances in Toronto as temperatures hovered around 100 degrees Fahrenheit (33 degrees Celsius) inside the sold-out Maple Leaf Gardens. As the Beatles tried to make their fast getaway at the end of the concert, a girl managed to get on stage and clung to George, sobbing. According to the *Toronto Star*, "She was disentangled with difficulty."

"It's like preparations for a full-scale, all-out war," the concert promoter told the *Atlanta Constitution*. They played to a crowd of 30,000 at the brand new Atlanta Stadium, home of the Braves baseball team. Brian told the paper that the Beatles enjoyed this performance more than any other because "they enjoyed being heard and hearing themselves for a change." This was attributed to the excellent sound system, which overcame the hysterical screams.

"Please Scream For Me"

Despite the 1 am arrival time, there were 2,000 fans at the airport in Houston to greet the Beatles. A radio station had leaked the arrival information, which caught the police unprepared to handle the crowd. Many fans managed to get past the police and close to the plane while it was taxiing. Some even managed to climb onto the wings and tap on the windows. The plane was forced to stop and wait until it was safe to continue. "Terrified," said Ringo when asked about the incident at the press conference. A psychiatrist interviewed by the *Houston Post* said, "A lot of parents are secret Beatles fans." He added, "Parents want to get out and do some yelling and screaming of their own, but are limited by society." He concluded, "When they let the kids go see the Beatles, they are enjoying it vicariously."

A well-behaved crowd of over 50,000 watched the Beatles perform for two shows at the White Sox Park in Chicago despite the hysteria. In Minneapolis they got away from the stadium in a laundry truck. A reporter for the *Minneapolis Tribune* put on a waitress' uniform at their hotel and waited for the call to room service for some food from the Beatles room. She delivered the food to them, revealed her true identity, and chatted with them for a while.

Prior to arriving in Portland, one of the planes engines bellowed thick black smoke. The firefighters took care of it as soon as the plane landed safely. It was quite a frightening experience for everyone. It was reported that John joked, "Beatles, women and children off first." During their visit, they met Brian Wilson and Mike Love of the Beach Boys backstage. *The Oregon Journal* reported, "One girl threw a wrapped mint which glanced off the head of Paul McCartney and landed deep in the stage area. After seeing the mint hit Paul, she fainted. After the performance, she pleaded for its return and the stage manager and a Portland policeman searched for the mint and as they returned it to her, she promptly collapsed again."

An Audience with the King

The Beatles rented a mansion in Beverly Hills to relax for a few days in private during a short break in their schedule. The secret didn't last long as their location was leaked to the fans by local radio stations and many gathered outside grounds of the mansion. Some even camped out on the surrounding hills with binoculars, hoping to get a glimpse. Throughout the mania, many fans had found very creative and sometimes dangerous means to get close to the

Beatle Bits

The Beatles Cartoons

In September 1965, a weekly series of animated cartoons began to air on American television featuring the Beatles. Every Saturday morning, millions of kids tuned in for half an hour to watch the adventures of John, Paul, George, and Ringo. Since the Beatles' Liverpudlian accents would have been difficult for many American children to understand, actors' voices were used. Original Beatles songs were included in the show. The series was syndicated around the world. In the fall of 1968, the series was moved to Sunday mornings where it remained until its final broadcast in the fall of 1969. This cartoon series was one of the first produced about living people

Beatles. During their stay in Beverly Hills, a helicopter hovering above the house suddenly began to descend over the swimming pool and when it got quite low, three fans jumped out into the water. Fortunately they weren't hurt and were promptly escorted off the property.

The Beatles met many Hollywood and music celebrities at a party, but the one they really wanted to meet wasn't there - Elvis. Although Elvis lived in Memphis, Tennessee, he had a home in Beverly Hills and he happened to be there at that time. So Brian made arrangements for the Beatles to visit him at his home. A couple of days later, the anxious Beatles and their entourage went to his place and finally got to meet him, something they'd wanted to do for a long time. They spent the evening talking and playing the guitar. To have the biggest stars of pop music together was a significant occasion. The Beatles called it one of the highlights of their career.

Human Avalanche

After the brief break, the Beatles continued with the tour and performed in San Diego. Then they went back to Los Angeles and played two shows at the Hollywood Bowl. For their final and perhaps most memorable appearance of the tour, they went to San Francisco. Unfortunately it was memorable for all the wrong reasons. *The San Francisco Chronicle* headline summed it up, "Beatles Play S.F. as a Riot Rages." The paper wrote, "It started with the jelly beans, bouncing like tracer bullets off the electric guitars. Then Beatle Harrison got hit with a flying blue teddy bear, Beatle McCartney dodged a paper airplane. Then the flowers, more jelly beans and finally the human avalanche."

The police were losing control of the crowd and the show was stopped as fans began to rush the stage. Paul pleaded with fans, but to no avail. He quickly left the stage. "By now the whole of the stage area was in complete chaos. Unconscious teenagers were plucked from beneath the surging mass and dragged across the stage," the London *Daily Mirror* reported. When order was restored, the Beatles returned and hastily finished their performance. At a press conference between shows, the Beatles expressed their dismay at the lack of security that allowed the crowds to rush the stage and place everyone in danger. To prevent a recurrence of the problem, barricades were placed in front of the stage for the next show. The following day, a columnist for the San Francisco Chronicle suggested that the Beatles might never play in San Francisco again due to the problems they encountered.

When the Beatles returned to Britain, Paul commented that the tour was wild and that they had reached the point where they didn't care if Beatlemania faded the next day. It was quite obvious they were exhausted and that the problems related to their tour were taking a toll on them. Even while at home they had frequent photo sessions, interviews with the press, appearances on television and radio shows to promote their songs, and invitations to every conceivable charity event. All the while churning out records literally on command. Everybody wanted a piece of them. They rarely had a moment to themselves. George said that the only place they got some peace was when they locked themselves in the bathroom!

In just two years, they had recorded five chart-topping albums, released ten singles, filmed two movies, appeared on hundreds of television and radio programs, and had traveled tens-of thousands of miles to perform in dozens of cities globally. This non-stop schedule had allowed them very little personal time and they believed it was affecting their professional development. There was no doubt they were drowning in the wave of Beatlemania. As usual, Brian had lined up numerous events for them over the upcoming months. The Beatles met with Brian and citing the need for some time off, declined most of them. They also wanted to spend more time in the studio and work on new material over the next few months. They did agree, however, to a very short tour of Britain near the end of the year and a few personal appearances. To limit the number of personal appearances promoting new songs and albums, they also agreed to tape promotional videos to be shown on television, sowing the seeds for music videos and MTV.

7

Tomorrow Never Knows

Seeds of Change

By autumn 1965, it had been two years since Beatlemania erupted in Britain, followed by the conquest of America and the rest of the world. The Beatles turned the music industry up side down everywhere they went, opening the door for new acts to follow suit. British groups such as the Rolling Stones, the Byrds, and Herman's Hermits, among others, were making their own mark in America and the rest of the world. Beatlemania re-invigorated American music artists with Bob Dylan, the Beach Boys, and the Supremes leading the way. The proliferation of new artists intensified the rivalry between artists, and resulted in producing much better music as the post-war generation was maturing along with the music.

Folk-rock was leading a cultural revolution among American youth; particularly with university students as more and more were speaking up against the war in Vietnam and racial segregation in the southern United States. Harder-edged rock music was also carving its own niche with the youth. Illegal drug use among teenagers was becoming more prevalent. The generation gap between teenagers and their parents was growing wider as more parents found themselves alienated from their adolescent children. Boundaries of acceptable behavior by teenagers were on the verge of being stretched beyond imagination in an attempt to assert their independence. Many of these changes were spreading all around the world.

The Beatles, well aware of the changes going on around them, were also undergoing a change. Beatlemania had taken an immense toll on the four young men and affected every aspect of their lives. They had to grow up very fast. Every move they made was scrutinized and publicized for the world to see. Many times hurtful, incorrect things were written about them. Two of them had families to take care of. The pressures they felt were common among celebrities, but at least as musicians, the Beatles had an outlet: their music.

Rubber Soul

The Beatles, still avid fans of a variety of styles of music, took every opportunity to listen to new music. They found their musical influences were also changing. Contemporaries such as Bob Dylan, the Beach Boys and the Byrds garnered their admiration and attention while fueling the Beatles' desire to be better than them. This and their own personal challenges were pushing them in a new musical

Above: Front cover of *Rubber Soul*

Below: *Rubber Soul* song list.

THE BEATLES

RUBBER SOUL

ADD
CDP 7 46440 2
(DIDX 1491)

1. **DRIVE MY CAR**
   (Lennon/McCartney)
2. **NORWEGIAN WOOD (This Bird Has Flown)**
   (Lennon/McCartney)
3. **YOU WON'T SEE ME**
   (Lennon/McCartney)
4. **NOWHERE MAN**
   (Lennon/McCartney)
5. **THINK FOR YOURSELF**
   (Harrison)
6. **THE WORD**
   (Lennon/McCartney)
7. **MICHELLE**
   (Lennon/McCartney)
8. **WHAT GOES ON**
   (Lennon/McCartney/Starkey)
9. **GIRL**
   (Lennon/McCartney)
10. **I'M LOOKING THROUGH YOU**
    (Lennon/McCartney)
11. **IN MY LIFE**
    (Lennon/McCartney)
12. **WAIT**
    (Lennon/McCartney)
13. **IF I NEEDED SOMEONE**
    (Harrison)
14. **RUN FOR YOUR LIFE**
    (Lennon/McCartney)

 ℗ 1965 Original Sound Recordings made by EMI Records Ltd
© 1965 EMI Records Ltd

COMPACT
disc
DIGITAL AUDIO
PRINTED IN U.S.A.

direction at the risk of alienating their core fans of young teenage girls and the uncertainty of whether they could capture the interest of a more mature audience. This was a pivotal point in their career.

Every new album they recorded demonstrated progress in their development as singers, songwriters and musicians. The Beatles were never afraid of breaking new ground and that's exactly what they did in *Rubber Soul*. This album is viewed as the one that began their transition from an energetic live club band to a more sophisticated studio band. Although they channeled their talents to more introspective, intellectual songs dealing with love, life and relationships, they still managed to generate some catchy pop tunes reminiscent of their early days. This formula continued throughout the rest of the band's career.

The resulting album contained different styles of music with something for everyone. This album also began their transition from focusing on producing hit singles to producing complete albums. It also marked the beginning of when the Beatles started writing all the songs recorded on their albums. Ringo got his first songwriting credit with John and Paul on "What Goes On," marking the first time all four Beatles were credited as songwriters on one album. George had two songs on the album. He had also become aware of the Indian sitar during the filming of *Help!* and played it on John's "Norwegian Wood (This Bird Has Flown)," a first on an English language record. Paul's love ballad "Michelle" mixed in some French lyrics, while John's reflective "In My Life," reminiscing his past has been proclaimed by many as one of the best songs ever written.

Rubber Soul was released in December 1965 and soared to the top of the charts. The American version, as usual, contained fewer songs, but also topped the charts. Fans, critics and their contemporaries in music all raved about the album. The Beatles had started to move on to a

George Harrison with his new bride, Pattie.

new chapter in their career. They embarked on a short tour of Britain, which included a concert in Liverpool, performing several songs from their new album.

In January 1966 George married Pattie Boyd, the woman he met while filming *A Hard Day's Night,* leaving Paul as the only bachelor in the group. It wasn't until April 1966 that the Beatles returned to the studio to record the next album, *Revolver.* The Beatles continued to stay away from major appearances and declined to make another movie.

Revolver

Over the years, the Beatles had taken an interest in the production end of the recording process, learning as much as they could. Because of the non-stop schedule, however, they rarely had any time to spend in the studio. With *Rubber Soul* they had a little bit more time, but it was completed fairly quickly. As technological advances in recording techniques emerged, they were very intrigued in some of the new sounds that could be produced. They persuaded George Martin to let them try out some of the innovations in their records. The result was an album with experimental and innovative production techniques combined with remarkable songwriting that exceeded expectations and influenced many of their contemporaries.

Improvements in George's songwriting skills were quite apparent in this album with three songs credited to him. Of all the Beatles, George was the most financially astute in the early years. Unhappy that the government was taking most of the money he was earning, he wrote "Taxman" to voice his disapproval. George's interest in Indian music had grown quite a bit and he wrote "Love to You" with Indian instruments combined with acoustic guitars in mind. Indian musicians were brought in to play

Above: Front cover of *Revolver*

Below: *Revolver* song list.

1	**TAXMAN** (Harrison)
2	**ELEANOR RIGBY** (Lennon/McCartney)
3	**I'M ONLY SLEEPING** (Lennon/McCartney)
4	**LOVE YOU TO** (Harrison)
5	**HERE, THERE AND EVERYWHERE** (Lennon/McCartney)
6	**YELLOW SUBMARINE** (Lennon/McCartney)
7	**SHE SAID SHE SAID** (Lennon/McCartney)
8	**GOOD DAY SUNSHINE** (Lennon/McCartney)
9	**AND YOUR BIRD CAN SING** (Lennon/McCartney)
10	**FOR NO ONE** (Lennon/McCartney)
11	**DOCTOR ROBERT** (Lennon/McCartney)
12	**I WANT TO TELL YOU** (Harrison)
13	**GOT TO GET YOU INTO MY LIFE** (Lennon/McCartney)
14	**TOMORROW NEVER KNOWS** (Lennon/McCartney)

COMPACT disc DIGITAL AUDIO | AAD CDP 7 46441 (DIDX 1481)

Recording Produced by George Martin
Engineer: Geoff Emerick

℗ 1966 Original Sound Recordings made :MI Records L
© 1966 ⁻MI Records Ltd.

apple records

PARLOPHONE

the sitar and tabla (Indian drums) while Ringo played the tambourine.

"Eleanor Rigby" is a depiction of loneliness. Paul originally believed that he got the idea for the title from the name of Eleanor Bron, the actress who starred in *Help!* Rigby, Paul thought, came from a store that he had visited. Later it was discovered that the name "Eleanor Rigby" was marked on a gravestone at the cemetery at the church where John and Paul met. Paul wondered if he may have seen the gravestone as a child and the name was subconsciously lodged in his memory.

Only the Beatles could pull off a children's song in their album. Paul, liked children and their imagination, wrote "Yellow Submarine" for Ringo to sing. They had a lot of fun recording the sound effects for the song and used everyone working in and around the studio to sing the chorus. "Tomorrow Never Knows" was a song about meditation written by John, but the meaning gets lost in the most unusual sound the recording techniques created. Experimenting with simple, yet brilliant techniques with the basic tape machine, the song was a prelude to the psychedelic era that was on the horizon. The title was another one of Ringo's malapropisms.

"Paperback Writer" and "Rain" were both recorded during the *Revolver* sessions, but were released as a single, giving the public a taste of what was to come in the upcoming album. The single quickly went to number one. The album was released in August 1966 and quickly topped the charts. It was a critical and commercial success. Once again, the Beatles had forged into new territory, risking alienating some of their fans, but succeeding in attracting more fans.

8

It's All Too Much

From Hamburg to Tokyo

Almost six months after their last tour, the Beatles left for another ambitious tour taking them to Germany, Japan and the Philippines in June 1966. For the first time since 1962, they returned to Germany and received a rousing welcome by thousands in the streets and played to sold-out arenas. They opened in Munich and then traveled by a special luxury train, previously used for British royalty, to the city of Essen and finally to Hamburg. Returning to Hamburg was quite sentimental for them as they recalled the old days of working long hours for little pay, but still having fun. The "old days" were only four to six years ago, but felt like decades. They got a chance to meet privately with several of their old friends from the clubs. They also spent some time with Astrid Kirchherr, Stu's fiancée before his death.

On their way to Japan, they had to detour to Alaska for a day because of a typhoon warning in Japan. It turned out to be a nice diversion for the Beatles as they enjoyed the natural beauty of the land. Although they arrived in Tokyo at 3:30 am, there were about 1,500 fans at the airport and that was after police convinced many to go home before the Beatles arrived. According to the English language *Japan Times*, school authorities had warned students to remain in school during the Beatles' appearances in Tokyo or be severely punished, including the threat of expulsion from school. The police were warned, "to watch out for boys and girls running away from schools and homes because thousands of them are reportedly ardent Beatles fans."

The Beatles, scheduled to play five concerts at the historic Nippon Budokan Hall, found themselves under extremely heavy security due to death threats against them. The hall was regarded as a national shrine to the war dead and used primarily for traditional martial arts performances, thus upsetting some people because rock and roll would be performed there. Tokyo, like Hong Kong, was considered a shopper's paradise, but the Beatles were unable to go out and shop, so vendors came to their hotel with merchandise.

Prior to their arrival, the concert tickets were sold only to those selected in a drawing from entries sent to a sponsoring newspaper. More than 200,000 entries were received. During the concerts, the fans were under the watchful eye of the large, gray clad, white-capped police force inside the hall. The fans could scream and wave their handkerchiefs, but were not allowed to stand up. Nothing came about from the death threats and, except for a few protestors outside, their reception was very warm. The

Beatles were very impressed with the way their entire visit in Japan had been organized by the Japanese and the politeness of the teenaged fans. Everything was well planned and even the fans co-operated with the police. During their drive back to the airport, fans gathered only at designated locations along the street to wave to the Beatles.

The *Japan Times* reported that Japanese language newspapers criticized the "excessive security precautions" at the hotel and airport that made it difficult for many fans to see the Beatles. There were a reported 300 policemen around the hotel and 1,000 at the airport to control the crowd of 2,000 fans on hand to say goodbye to the Beatles.

Escape from Manila

Three days prior to the Beatles' arrival in the Philippines, the *Manila Times* reported that "the tightest security measures since U.S President Eisenhower's state visit" were planned. On the day of their arrival, the paper reported that the Beatles planned to visit the First Lady, Imelda Marcos, the following morning. Thousands waited their arrival, but didn't get more than a glimpse. Upon their arrival, the Beatles were shocked to find themselves separated from their carry-on luggage as well as from other members of their entourage, as the heavily armed security guards hustled them into a limo and quickly drove them away. They were driven to the city marina, put on a small boat and taken to a yacht anchored out in the harbor. For the first time since their early days, they were without Neil, Mel, Brian and the others who normally protected them. Not knowing what was going on, they were quite concerned as armed guards surrounded the cabin they were waiting in. After a few anxious hours, everything was sorted out and the Beatles were taken to their hotel. They said it was one of the most frightening experiences of their lives. It was rumored that the yacht owner, a wealthy and well-connected person, had them taken to his yacht so his friends could meet the Beatles privately.

The following morning, the Beatles were awakened by someone banging on the door and told that they were late for their lunch appointment with the First Lady and her guests who were waiting at the Presidential Palace. The Beatles were surprised to hear about that, but weren't prepared to go. It is unclear what caused the mix-up because Brian had previously turned down the invitation and did not say anything about it to the Beatles. The Beatles had stopped accepting invitations for receptions and meetings with politicians and other local dignitaries because it had simply become an autographing session. They preferred to give autographs to their real fans, but fan frenzy had made that difficult.

When the hotel room service would not bring their breakfast up to their room, they turned on the television and watched in disbelief as the news broadcasted live reports from the Presidential palace about the Beatles not showing up. That afternoon and evening the Beatles played two concerts before a crowd of about 80,000 combined, though it is believed tens of thousands of additional fans got in illegally. On the way back to the hotel, they sensed something was wrong, as most of the security normally afforded them had been withdrawn.

The following morning the headlines in the paper read, "Imelda Stood Up. First Family Waits in Vain for Mopheads." Another headline for an article reviewing the concerts said, "They Were Terrific." As they prepared to depart to the airport, they found the hotel staff very discourteous and once again they were left without security. They had difficulty getting transportation to the airport. At the airport a large group of angry people screamed and yelled insults to the Beatles. Left without any security, the

BEATLES, GO HOME!

That was the chant as an airport crowd jostled and jeered the boys in 'snub' row

One of the Beatles' party, Alf Bicknell, is helped up after a fall caused by a kick on the leg.

NEVER before has anything remotely like this happened to the Beatles.

Up to yesterday, they could be called the most feted young men in the world, acclaimed with frenzied enthusiasm wherever they went.

Yesterday there was frenzy . . . but of anger and hate.

The Beatles were jostled, booed and jeered in a hectic airport scene at Manila, capital of the Philippines, as they left for their homeward trip by way of New Delhi.

Fists were shaken at them. Screwed-up pieces of paper were thrown at them.

And there were shouts of "Beatles, Go Home!" . . . "Go to Hell!" . . . "Get out of our country!" . . . and "We don't want you here!"

About 200 angry Fili-

pinos — young and old—staged this unprecedented demonstration against the Beatles. They were smarting, under an alleged snub to Senora Imelda Marcos, wife of their President.

Many Filipinos, including the Press, were upset when John, Ringo, Paul and George failed to appear as invited to meet Senora Marcos at the palace on Monday.

Regrets

The Beatles said that they knew nothing about the invitation.

And last night the President and his wife issued a statement regretting the airport incidents.

They added: "There was no intention on the part of the Beatles to slight the first lady or the Government."

But, earlier, the crowd at the airport had thought otherwise.

After the Beatles arrival at the airport, an angry crowd grew round them. Within minutes people were pushing them.

One of the party, Alf Bicknell, fell after being kicked in the leg.

A radio reporter who got near the Beatles said that a Filipino swung a wild right at Ringo Starr—but missed. By contrast with

their arrival, the departure of the Beatles was officially brusque and without any VIP treatment.

The group had to carry their baggage up to the second floor themselves. The power for the special escalator had been turned off.

Almost all police protection and special arrangements were cancelled—and the tax office announced that the Beatles could not leave the Philippines until they had made a declaration of their earnings.

The Beatles themselves were bewildered. As they walked to their airliner, Paul McCartney exclaimed disconsolately:

THEY TREATED US LIKE ANIMALS, SAYS RINGO

A bewildering moment . . . reflected in the expression of John Lennon (in the background, right) amid a jostling crowd. Ringo Starr is in the foreground—and on the left is the Beatles' road manager, Neil Aspinall.

"Man, I don't understand!" CONSOLATION awaited the Beatles in a tumultuous and joyous welcome at New Delhi airport last night. Again they were pushed, shoved and pelted —but with garlands.

"They treated us like animals where we just came from," Ringo Starr told 600 Indian fans.

"We never meant to upset anybody by not attending the party. It was all fixed up for us to go—but the only thing was that nobody told us."

Beatles and their entourage were jostled as they made their way through the airport. Fortunately, no one was seriously injured. Alf Bicknell, their driver and bodyguard, got the worst of it when a kick to his shin knocked him down. Despite the hostile crowd, a small group of fans courageously showed their support for the Beatles. As they were about to leave, the plane was held up as Brian and a couple of others with the entourage were summoned off the plane. They returned after a short time and told the others that they had to pay an enormous amount of 'tax' to the official. It amounted to their entire earnings from the concerts. In a statement from the Presidential Press Office a couple of days later, President Ferdinand Marcos expressed regret over the incident at the airport and said it was a "breach of Filipino hospitality." The Beatles never blamed the Philippine fans, just the corrupt government officials. The money was never returned.

On their way back to London, the Beatles had a planned stopover in New Delhi, India for a couple of days because George wanted to purchase a sitar. After the Manila fiasco, however, they just wanted to go home, but were unable to change their flights. Fortunately, it turned out to be a welcome respite after Manila. To their surprise, word had leaked out about their arrival even though this was a private visit and hundreds of fans gathered at the airport to greet them. The Beatles had thought that at least in this ancient land they would get away without being recognized. George commented, "Foxes have holes and birds have nests, but the Beatles have nowhere to lay their heads." They managed to elude the fans at the hotel and got out to do some shopping and sightseeing. The Indian culture made quite an impact on George. He said India was an incredible place that "bombards your senses" with all the sounds and colors. He was astonished at the contrasts in the life there with the extremes in both wealth and poverty.

Alabama Burning

In an extensive, candid interview with Maureen Cleave of the *London Evening Standard* in early 1966, John Lennon discussed several topics surrounding his life, including religion. She wrote that he had been reading extensively about religion and quoted him saying, "We're more popular than Jesus." She also mentioned that "he paused over objects he still fancies: a huge altar crucifix of a Roman Catholic nature" and "an enormous Bible he bought." Readers, be wary that unless you read the entire article and the context within which he discussed religion, it is easy to rush to an incorrect judgment about the quote above. Unfortunately, that's exactly what happened when in July, an American teen magazine, *DATEbook*, reprinted some quotes out of context as a part of a front cover story entitled "The Ten Adults You Dig/Hate the Most."

This caught the attention of a radio station in Birmingham, Alabama. They called for a boycott of the Beatles and organized public bonfires to burn Beatles products and ban their music from the radio. Many stations across the country, particularly in the southern United States, known to be very religious and referred to as the Bible belt, began to heed the call. The boycott quickly spread world wide as a radio station in Spain as well the South African Broadcasting Corporation, a state-run national network stopped playing Beatles music. All of this was happening just days before the Beatles were about to set upon another concert tour of the United States. There were death threats made against the Beatles and protests were planned when they toured. Yet, the article, published several months earlier in Britain, didn't cause any kind of reaction there.

In order to diffuse the situation, Brian flew to New York and met with reporters and concert promoters and said that John was misinterpreted and was just commenting on the regrettable decline of Christianity, especially among the youth. Brian failed to quell the outcry. So far, John had not commented publicly on this matter. Ironically, the Beatles had a concert scheduled in the Bible belt city of Memphis, Tennessee, home to Elvis. Some support was shown for the Beatles. Several radio stations announced they would continue playing Beatles records regardless of the comments. A radio station in Kentucky, located in the Bible belt, announced that they would begin playing Beatles records for the first time because they felt those banning them were being hypocrites. *The New York Times* quoted a reverend from Wisconsin who said, "Those outraged by the remarks should start blaming themselves and stop blaming the Beatles. There is much validity in what Lennon said. To many people today, the golf course is also more popular than Jesus Christ."

There was some discussion about canceling the tour or just canceling the Memphis stop, but they decided to go on as planned. A few days later, the Beatles arrived in Chicago for their first concert of the tour and met as customary with the press. As expected, the reporters pressed John about his comments. Part of what he said was, "If I had said television is more popular than Jesus, I might have got away with it. I'm not saying that we're better, or greater, or comparing us with Jesus Christ as a person or God as a thing. I just said 'they' (the Beatles) are having more influence on kids and things than anything else, including Jesus. I never meant it to be anti-religious." He apologized that it had offended some people, but continued to insist that he had been misinterpreted. John had to repeat these comments to reporters over and over again throughout the concert tour.

The concerts in Chicago and Detroit went on without any major incidents. In Cleveland, the rush of the

Radio station disc jockey's tearing up Beatles albums in protest of John's Jesus comments.

Beatle Bits

South Africa was the only country to officially ban Beatles music and items because of John's comments. It was rumored, however, that the ban was primarily because the Beatles turned down appearances in South Africa due to the country's apartheid policy, which legally discriminated against people of color. The ban remained in effect for several years. Apartheid ended in 1989.

A lightning strike knocked a Texas radio station off the air the day after it organized a bon-fire to burn Beatles records.

fans flattened a protective fence around the infield of the baseball stadium and some fans even made it to the stage. The concert was stopped for twenty minutes until order was restored. In Washington, the *Washington Star* reported that, "A small band of five Ku Klux Klansmen paraded near the stadium, but created no disturbances." Fans wearing "I STILL love the Beatles" buttons were spotted in Philadelphia where the Beatles snuck in and out of the stadium in a flower truck. In Toronto, 167 fans were administered first aid and in Boston, some family members of the former President Kennedy were in attendance.

Due to the threats against the Beatles in Memphis, security was very tight. "The tightest security we've had to handle for a show in Memphis," a police official was quoted as saying in *The Memphis Commercial Appeal*. A Ku Klux Klan spokesperson appeared on television threatening a 'surprise,' but only six people wearing white robes picketed outside the Coliseum. They handed out anti-Beatles material and carried signs protesting Lennon's comments. "Anyone leaving his seat during either of the shows will be ejected," the Coliseum management announced prior to the concert. The first show was delayed because of a bomb threat. A couple of firecrackers or cherry bombs were set off during the second shows near the stage, but the Beatles didn't miss a note. Two teenagers were arrested as police found a sack with twenty-five cherry bombs and a purse with twenty-five firecrackers in their possession. The Beatles were relieved to leave Memphis in one piece. It appeared that the uproar was relegated to a small number of people and radio stations, but the heavy press coverage made it seem to be much larger than it really was. Regardless, it had a major effect on the emotional state of the Beatles.

Rain postponed the Beatles concert in Cincinnati until noon the following day and rain threatened to do the same in St. Louis that evening, but they played through the rain because the stage had a canopy to keep the electrical equipment safe. The Beatles returned to Shea Stadium and played to a crowd of 45,000 before heading to Seattle. A 13-year-old blind girl wrote about her experience at the Beatles concert for *The Seattle Times*. She wrote, "Before the Beatles arrived on stage we were treated to the music of four groups which have yet to attain the Beatles' fame. The audience response was lukewarm. Just before the Beatles' appearance, the suspense was as great as that preceding the opening of presents on Christmas morning. Then they were there! I knew because the screams reached a pitch that was both terrifying and exciting."

Flames out at Candlestick

The Beatles played at Dodger Stadium in Los Angeles in front of a crowd of 45,000. Due to crowd control problems, they were unable to leave the stadium for quite some time. At last they were on their way to their final stop of the tour at Candlestick Park in San Francisco. Due to the city's history of crowd control problems, elaborate preparations were made to avoid trouble this time, including a double row of fencing in front of the stage and increased police presence to keep fans in the stands a hundred feet away from the stage. This resulted in a relatively trouble-free concert and turned out to be a good ending to a very demanding tour. The Beatles were glad to be going home again. While they didn't sell out everywhere, they still drew more fans in total than they did in the previous year because they played in larger venues.

August 29, 1966, is another date etched in Beatles history, as it turned out that the concert in San Francisco was their last paid public performance ever. Nobody knew it at that time - not even the Beatles. The Beatles had been talking amongst themselves for a while about not touring again, but they really didn't know what the future held. They had probably given a couple of thousand performances over the past nine or ten years as they had been performing since they were teenagers. Beatlemania, while great for the most part, had its drawbacks with the uncontrollable frenzy it created endangering not just the Beatles, but also the fans themselves. Near misses with dangerously sharp objects thrown at them, albeit with affection, death threats, press conferences, grueling travel schedules as well as the events like those in the Philippines and Memphis had taken everything the Beatles could give. They just could not give any more of themselves. Recording *Rubber Soul* and *Revolver* had given them a taste of studio life and they knew that that this was what they really wanted to do.

When they returned to Britain, they took about three months off. George went to India to learn more about the Indian culture and also to improve his skills on the sitar. Ravi Shankar, the world's greatest sitar player taught him. They had met for the first time in London just prior to the 1966 tour. George, with his wife, Pattie, had a great time in India, shopping, sightseeing and even learning the art of yoga while staying on a houseboat in the foothills of the Himalayas. George also began to learn about meditation and picked up several books on Indian spiritual philosophy. He said that he felt "very liberated" because of his experience in India.

John went to Spain to take part in a movie called *How I Won the War*, an anti-war satire. Paul and George Martin wrote and orchestrated music for a film called, *The Family Way*. Paul also went on an African safari to Kenya. Ringo spent the time with Maureen and baby Zak and also visited John in Spain for a while.

The press constantly brought up rumors of a break-up during this time off. The Beatles continually denied it whenever the press caught up with them. Many reports said the Beatles were finished and could never surpass what they had already accomplished. The Beatles reconvened near the end of November to begin work on what was going to be the most ambitious artistic project they had ever tackled. Once again, the Beatles were about to make pop music history.

Beatle Bits

The New Musical Express (NME), a national music publication, annually polled its readers to select the top artists of the year. To honor the winners, the publication sponsored a celebration concert featuring those artists. The Beatles had been a regular feature since 1963. (The poll had been conducted in 1962 and the Beatles were unknown then, but because their popularity soared in 1963, they were invited as guests for the concert). Their appearance at the May 1, 1966 NME concert was their last live public concert in Britain. Other notable artists performing were the Rolling Stones, the Yardbirds (with Eric Clapton), the Who, and Roy Orbison.

The Beatles, as they frequently did, made their way into the stadium in a disguise. Led by Ringo and disguised as chefs, they carried trays of cakes and ran through the kitchen to get backstage. Unfortunately, Ringo tripped and fell, scattering cakes all over the place while the other Beatles landed on top! Fortunately, no one was hurt and they had a good laugh about it.

9

Kaleidoscope Eyes

Salt and Pepper

During the time off in the autumn of 1966, each Beatle spent a great deal of time reflecting upon the events of that year and pondering the future of the band. Despite the controversies they had faced, *Rubber Soul* and *Revolver* had given them great faith in their ability to continue to develop and improve creatively. These albums had brought in a new audience for their music, primarily older teenagers and college students. They could not, however, shake the image they had developed early on as teenage idols and "mop tops," a title referring to their hairstyle.

On his way back home from the safari in Africa, Paul contemplated this problem. He came up with an idea to develop alter egos for the Beatles. He thought it would be interesting to actually take on the personas of a different band. The intent was that even though it would be the Beatles writing, playing, and singing, they would portray themselves as a fictional band in the hopes that it would shed their old image: a difficult concept to grasp and even more difficult to pull it off.

Many bands around that time had odd names like Quicksilver Messenger Service and Big Brother and the Holding Company. Paul liked the idea of this type of name for the band. Paul said that he was joking around with Mal Evans about the 'S' and 'P' on salt and pepper shakers and called them "Sergeant Pepper." He then added Lonely Hearts Club Band to it to come up with "Sgt. Pepper's Lonely Hearts Club Band" for the band name. That also became the name of their next album.

The design of the album was unique for that time period. The Beatles were dressed in old-fashioned military band uniforms as members of Sgt. Pepper's band on the cover. The front cover included nearly seventy famous and not-so-famous writers, actors, comedians, and other personalities, notably: Albert Einstein, Bob Dylan, Shirley Temple, and former Beatle Stuart Sutcliff. Ironically, it also included wax figures of the Beatles as they looked in the early days of Beatlemania. It was the first album to include all the lyrics to the songs, covering the entire back of the album. It was also the first album cover to open like a book. Cardboard cutouts of a moustache, stripes, badges, and other small items were also included inside the album. The originality and artistic expression of the album cover was considered an opening for other artists to create their own artistic impression.

Above: Front cover of *Sergeant Pepper's Lonely Heart Club Band* album.

Below: *Sergeant Pepper's Lonely Heart* Club Band song listing.

A Splendid Time is Guaranteed for All

When the recording sessions began for the album, the Beatles told George Martin that they wanted to experiment even more with a variety of recording techniques than they did in *Revolver* because they wanted this album to be very different. They spent a great deal of time in the studio working with George Martin on every aspect of the recording process, reaching a level of sophistication unheard of in pop music. George Martin found that John and Paul had developed different techniques when recording their songs. Paul was very deliberate in what he wanted and was able to give George Martin very specific instructions. Paul also worked very closely with George Martin during the production of his songs. John, on the other hand, had conceptual ideas and let George Martin develop them to John's satisfaction. Sometimes this meant that George Martin would have to come up with a variety of options for John to consider. Both approaches led to a very time-consuming process of precise and deliberate recordings and re-recordings. A lot of time was taken to coach numerous session musicians to incorporate some of the unconventional styles the Beatles wanted in their songs. In addition, an assortment of sound effects ranging from animals to applause was added.

Therefore, it was no surprise that the album took nearly five months to record and resulted in what many critics and fans called "a masterpiece." *Time* magazine said that, "they have moved on to a higher artistic plateau" and "are creating the most original, expressive and musically interesting sounds being heard in pop music." Many of the Beatles contemporaries still refer to this album as their inspiration for musical and artistic progress. Not everyone was pleased with the new Beatles sound as some critics and many young fans lamented the loss of the old Mersey

George Martin, left with Paul McCartney in the studio.

sound. Others disliked it for being "overly sophisticated."

With this album, the transformation from the old to the new Beatles was complete. Beatlemania as the world knew it was gone. The new Beatles emerged with a new direction and a new sense of purpose, which was to do what they wanted to do, for their own enjoyment.

The first song recorded for the album, "Strawberry Fields Forever," never made it to the album because Brian was anxious to put out a single due to the slow progress with the album. "Penny Lane," also originally slated for the album, was selected for the other side of "Strawberry Fields Forever." This was a double A side as both John and Paul each felt that the song they had written deserved the A side, and rightfully so. Even though a song written primarily by

The Beatles promote *Sergeant Pepper's Lonely Heart Club Band* album.

either one was credited to both, there was healthy competition between them, which probably made them even more creative. Ironically, both songs were based on places in Liverpool. Strawberry Fields was a Salvation Army home for orphans near John's home where he and his friends had spent time on the large, treed grounds of the home. The song, however, does not relate to the home specifically, it's more of an imaginary trip you'd find in *Alice In Wonderland*, John's favorite book as a child. They recorded a slow and a slightly faster version of the song. John liked the beginning of the slow version and the ending of the faster one, so George Martin ended up combining the two versions. Listen to it and see if you can figure out where they were combined.

Paul takes us on a picturesque tour down memory lane in "Penny Lane," reminiscing about his childhood in Liverpool with a lot of play on words. *The London Times,* a very conservative newspaper, wrote an unprecedented editorial discussing the positive virtues of the song, calling it "delightful" and "original." These songs offered fans an excellent taste of the creativity, vivid imagery, and mystical sounds they could expect on the forthcoming album.

The album begins with the title track, which welcomes everyone to the imaginary concert by Sgt. Pepper's Band and added an applause sound effect, giving the illusion of a live show. It's reprised near the end of the album, thanking everyone for coming to the show. "Lucy in the Sky with Diamonds" caused some controversy as the acronym stood for an illegal drug. John, however, dispelled that notion by explaining that his young son, Julian, had brought home a drawing from school of a girl and a sky full of stars and it was titled "Lucy in the sky with diamonds." Paul wrote "When I'm Sixty Four" when he was just sixteen, but didn't record it until this album. "She's Leaving Home" is a poignant account of relationship struggles between teenagers and parents and was inspired by a newspaper article John and Paul read about a teenage girl running away from home.

A poster about an old-fashioned circus was the inspiration for John's "Being for the Benefit of Mr. Kite." He said that he simply connected most of the words on the poster for the lyrics in the song. John wanted some circus organ music generally heard on carousels, but of course, not quite so simplistic. George Martin tried using some of the new the technology to create something different with the sound of multiple electric organs, but it just didn't work. So he took the tape he had recorded, cut it up in pieces, mixed them up and taped them back together, creating an unusual, but magical circus sound. George, still into Indian music, brought in several Indian musicians to play on "Within You, Without You," which had a heavy spiritual emphasis. The album ended with "A Day in the Life," a dreamy song based on newspaper articles John had read about a car accident, among other things. An unfinished song by Paul was added to the middle of this song, suddenly changing its tempo, making it quite an unusual song. Many fans consider this song to be one of their finest. The original album had no breaks between songs on either side of the record, but the compact disc version does.

The album was released in June 1967 and immediately topped the charts everywhere. For the first time, upon the insistence of the Beatles, this was the only version released around the world so all the fans could hear it as they wanted them to hear it. To this day, *Sgt. Pepper's Lonely Hearts Club Band* remains one of their best selling albums and one of the all-time top selling albums in pop music.

Flower Power

Many who grew up in the 1960s regard 1967 as the year that defined the decade. The seeds of change planted in the early to mid-1960s were now in full bloom. The psychedelic, hippy, and "flower power" era was underway. As the Vietnam War raged and the civil rights movement gained momentum, peace and love was the theme that brought this generation together in peaceful protest in the United States. By the summer of 1967, generally referred to as the "summer of love," this sentiment had spread around the world.

San Francisco became the heart of this new movement as thousands of youths went there to find camaraderie, although many were disappointed as they observed excessive amounts of drugs being used everywhere. Even George and Paul dropped in for brief a visit and found the same. Many new bands emerged with the message of peace and love in their music, which appealed to this age group. Music festivals began to gain popularity. The largest of these was the Monterey Pop Festival, held near San Francisco, which drew about two hundred thousand fans over a three-day period in June. There were performances by very diverse groups of musicians and singers including the Mama's and Papa's, the Byrds, the Who, and sitar great, Ravi Shankar. The Beatles had turned down the invitation, but recommended a rising star, Jimi Hendrix, who went on to become very famous after that festival. Just prior to the festival and two days after the album *Sgt. Pepper's Lonely Hearts Club Band* was released, Jimi opened a concert at a small theatre in London with the title track from that album, and by chance, Paul was in attendance. Paul said he was honored by the performance. The success of the Monterey Pop Festival encouraged other festivals including Woodstock, held in upstate New York, which drew nearly half a million fans.

In a bid to promote world unity, the first live global television show called "Our World" was scheduled to broadcast around the world via a satellite link. About two-dozen countries participated in the show and each country selected someone or something they wanted to showcase. The British Broadcasting Corporation (BBC) asked the Beatles to represent Britain on the show. The Beatles would be shown in the process of recording a song. Of course, unlike the recent recording sessions that took several days for each song, this song had to be done in one quick session. John wrote "All You Need Is Love" to suit the mood of the times and to present a positive message. The lyrics were kept simple so that people in non-English speaking countries could understand.

Above: The Beatles promote Our World campaign holding all you need is love signs in several languages.

Below: The Beatles meet the Maharishi in London.

On June 25, 1967, the Beatles gathered at the studio for the live television broadcast. Mick Jagger of the Rolling Stones and Eric Clapton were among the several friends and family invited to join them as backup singers. An orchestra was also on hand for the background music. The studio was decorated with balloons and flowers. The atmosphere certainly reflected the "summer of love" era. An estimated 350 million people watched the show on five continents. George Martin deserved plenty of praise for coordinating the complex undertaking, which resulted in a very successful show. The response to the song was so great that the Beatles quickly put it out as a single and it quickly topped the charts everywhere.

Within You, Without You

Despite all the fame and fortune the Beatles had, they still found something missing in their lives: spiritual enlightenment. While they professed to believe in God, none of them were very fond of organized religion. When George and Pattie went to India, they found the Indian philosophy of spiritual awareness to be very appealing. George told the other Beatles about it and let them read an assortment of books he had collected on the topic. In August 1967, the Beatles attended a lecture in London given by a prominent Indian guru called Maharishi Mahesh Yogi. Maharishi was quite popular in Britain as there was a sizeable Indian population in Britain and he had also attracted interest from native Britons. India had been a British colony for many years until its independence in 1947 and there was quite a bit of cross-cultural influence from both countries.

The Beatles were very impressed with the Maharishi's philosophy about life and accepted his invitation to attend a seminar he was giving on meditation

Social gathering at Maharishi's seminar in Bangor

in Bangor, a small town near Liverpool. There were many celebrities in attendance. Even the press was invited. After learning more about meditation and trying it out, the Beatles were fascinated by the results and even publicly promoted the virtues of meditation versus using drugs.

In the midst of the seminar, they received some devastating news. Brian had died. He had apparently accidentally overdosed on sleeping tablets at his home in London. The Beatles were devastated by the news. Brian was more than just their manager; he was their friend. He was a friend they had relied upon, a friend who had guided them. Brian was instrumental in their success. They received some valuable advice from the Maharishi that helped them cope with their grief and move on. They accepted Maharishi's invitation to his meditation academy in India for a three-month retreat, but delayed it until early 1968.

Daily Mirror

4d. Monday, August 28, 1967 ✦ No. 19,805

'NO WONDER THE MIRROR OUT-SELLS THE FIELD..'

BBC 'News-Stand' pays a remarkable tribute to the favourite daily newspaper of 15,756,000 readers

HAS any newspaper ever before been praised so highly by a completely independent commentator?

Here is a shortened version of what Mr. Brian Connell said about the Daily Mirror on the BBC's Home Service programme — News-Stand — on Friday:

"I will give you three guesses as to the source of these three extracts from these newspapers.

● "If Mr. Callaghan is sharply questioned about the way in which British wages and costs are rising after the freeze, he will be able to turn the question back and ask whether wages are not also going up in other countries, in America and the Continent of Europe. They are. But on the whole the Americans and the Continentals are justifying their higher pay by higher productivity. The fall in British industrial production since last year (index down from 135 to 133) suggests that the anticipated rise in wage rates this year is not being paid for by increased output. The position of the pound and the strength of the economy have improved since July last year. But it has been an improvement from near disaster. We are still precariously balanced on the tightrope."

Broadcaster Connell

BEARDED Brian Connell is the journalist who's often been called "the Richard Dimbleby of ITV."

In opposition to the formidable Dimbleby, he covered the wedding of Princess Alexandra and Mr. Angus Ogilvy at Westminster Abbey.

And it was Brian Connell who covered Sir Winston Churchill's funeral programme —which won for Independent Television the Cannes Film Festival Grand Prix Award for an outside broadcast.

For twenty-five years, Connell—who has also had several books published—worked as a journalist in Fleet-street.

Millions of TV viewers came to know him as a newscaster for ITV and for three years, as link-man for the ITV current affairs programme This Week.

Mr. Connell joined Anglia Television four years ago as programme adviser.

ELECTIONS

● "September 3 is voting day in the presidential elections in South Vietnam. Or it is for those who can escape the attentions of the Vietcong guerillas long enough to get to the polls. No one supposes that the elections will be fair. The winners, both military men, are known in advance. General Thieu, chief of state, will be President, and Nguyen Ky, the present Premier, will be the Vice-President. But at least some kind of elections are being held. Which is more than can be said for North Vietnam, where ruthless dictatorial ..."

◉ CONTINUED ON PAGE TWO

EPSTEIN
(The Beatle-Making Prince of Pop)
DIES AT 32

By TOM TULLETT and DAVID WRIGHT

BRIAN EPSTEIN, the man who made the Beatles, is dead.

The Quiet Prince of Pop, who built up a fantastic multi-million-pound show business empire, was found dead in bed at his £31,000 London home yesterday afternoon.

He was just thirty-two.

And last night a stunned Paul McCartney, one of the four Liverpool lads who made Epstein their friend, could say only:

"This is a great shock. I'm very upset."

Epstein, who always managed to ride the crest of the Merseyside pop wave, was found about 2.45 p.m. by his Spanish butler.

Bottles taken from his flat

The butler went to wake him in his second-floor bedroom at the three-storey terrace house in Chapel-street, Belgravia.

He knocked and knocked again. There was no reply. So the butler raised the alarm and went inside.

The room was in semi-darkness. The curtains were drawn. And Epstein was in bed.

The butler said later: "Mr. Epstein was alone in the house last night. He appeared to be quite well."

Commander John Lawler, head of the No. 1 district, Metropolitan Police, said: "We are treating this as a sudden death.

"There will probably be a post-mortem examination, but this is a matter for the coroner."

Unknown

And a spokesman for NEMS Enterprises — Epstein's firm that managed the Beatles, Cilla Black, Billy J. Kramer, Gerry and the Pacemakers, and other big pop names said:

"The reason for his death is unknown, but there were no untoward circumstances."

Several bottles and medicines were taken from the house, but there was said to be nothing to link

them with the cause of death.

Epstein's body left the house in a coffin about 5 p.m. And soon tributes from pop stars and fans began to flow in from all over the world.

The Beatles—who are in Bangor, North Wales, for the mass rally of a meditation society—made immediate plans to return to London.

First to leave were Paul and his girl friend, actress Jane Asher. She held his hand and wept.

John Lennon said: "Our meditation has given us confidence to withstand such a shock."

George Harrison said: "You cannot pay tribute in words. There is no such death as dying only to the physical sense. Life goes on. The important thing is that he is O.K. now."

Ringo said: "We owe a lot to Brian."

The Beatles were to have watched as Epstein was initiated at the meditation society's rally today.

A NEMS spokesman said: "The directors and everyone in the organisa-

THE QUIET MAN FROM LIVERPOOL WHO RAN A 'STABLE' OF STARS

◼ Continued on Back Page

First, they had to decide out how they were going to deal with a future without Brian. He had managed all their business affairs and left it to them to focus on the music. The Beatles realized that they knew very little about the business side of things and were quite concerned about it. Brian's younger brother, Clive, took over Brian's company, but the Beatles were not sure if they needed a manager like Brian anymore since they had stopped touring. They got together and decided that they would let the accountants and lawyers sort out the business matters and get their advice before deciding what to do.

The Walrus Was Paul

For a long time ideas for the next Beatles movie had been floating around, but the Beatles were not happy with any of them. None of them were too keen on spending several months making a movie and long hours on sets after their experience with *Help!* and *A Hard Day's Night.* They found it quite boring while waiting hours or even days between scenes. They had limited control and influence over the previous movies and wanted to be in charge. Therefore, they decided to make a short movie on their own and simply have fun. The idea to make their own short movie had been conceived prior to Brian's death and planning was already underway, so the Beatles decided that they would proceed with their plans.

When they were kids, John and Paul remembered being fascinated by the concept of mystery bus tours that took people on an excursion to unknown destinations. Many people took these tours just to have a party on the bus. Paul brought up the idea of renting a bus, gathering a group of people and going on an expedition with no particular destination in mind. They called it *Magical Mystery Tour.* They wanted it to be an unconventional,

Paul getting ready to head out on the Magical Mystery Tour bus.

wacky, slapstick kind of movie that relied more on actions than words. They made a basic plan of what some of the scenes would contain, but there was no detailed script. They were going to improvise as they went along. A bus full of passengers of all shapes and sizes was hired, including a few professional actors, who were quite apprehensive about working without a script or a rehearsal.

With a small technical crew, they took off on their journey really not knowing what to expect. The filming almost came to an abrupt halt when the bus got stuck on a very narrow bridge. Fortunately, they managed to free it with the help of the police and continued with the film. After a couple of madcap weeks, the filming was complete.

The Beatles added several music videos, some of which they had started making previously. The musical productions of John's "I am the Walrus" and Paul's "Your Mother Should Know" were quite outlandish in very different ways, reflecting the diverse styles of John and Paul. John had based "I am the Walrus" on a poem called "The Walrus and the Carpenter" by Lewis Carroll, author of *Alice in Wonderland*. The influence of *Alice in Wonderland* is very apparent in the movie, resulting in just what they intended: an unconventional, wacky, slapstick movie with an assortment of nonsensical and amusing characters. Since it was less than an hour long, they approached the BBC, which agreed to televise it nationally, but only after they censored a few scenes.

The expectations had been heightened by the time the movie aired on the day after Christmas. The response was one of surprise. The viewers were bewildered. A headline in the *Daily Mirror* read, "Mystery Tour Baffles Viewers." With no plot, no real direction, and what appeared to be a lot of haphazard skits, the critics lashed out at the Beatles. The following day, Paul was apologetic saying "maybe we goofed." He seemed to take it back, however, as he defended the movie itself, but admitted that perhaps showing such a movie on national television around Christmas was not the best idea and probably to the wrong audience. In addition, the movie was shown in black and white, which was unfortunate because color played a major role in the atmosphere of the movie. The BBC did rebroadcast it in color a week later, but only a very small percentage of the population had color television sets at that time. Over the years, the movie turned into a huge financial success, as several television networks around the world purchased rights to show it. Video sales, especially to young people, were tremendous. In some respects, it has gained a cult status because of its eccentric nature.

Above: Front cover of *Magical Mystery Tour*.

Below: *Magical Mystery Tour* song list.

Six new songs were introduced for the movie soundtrack including an instrumental number, "Flying," that was credited to John, Paul, George, and Ringo, the first time all four had received credit for the same song. Unlike *Sgt. Pepper,* there was more emphasis on the visual aspect of the musical productions and less emphasis on recording studio techniques. Since there weren't enough songs for an album, a double extended play (EP) was released in Britain: basically a mini-album. In the United States, however, a full album was released and included other recently released singles including "Strawberry Fields Forever" and "All You Need Is Love." The album quickly topped the charts.

1967 turned out to be quite an extraordinary year for the Beatles. From the incredible success of *Sgt. Pepper* to the death of Brian, from reaching out to the world with "All You Need Is Love" to the disapproving reaction to *Magical Mystery Tour,* it was a year of extremes. After leaving Beatlemania behind and giving up touring, this wasn't the kind of year they had expected. The upcoming retreat to India to practice meditation in tranquility couldn't have come at a better time.

Beatle Bits

During the summer of 1967, the Beatles went to Greece on vacation. While they were there, they considered buying an island where they all could live and get away from the intense scrutiny they faced on a daily basis. The Beatles found a small island they all liked and even went to the extent of having money sent to them from Britain. In the end, however, they did not go through with the idea. On another occasion, they considered buying a small English village just for themselves, but gave up on that idea too.

10

Inner Light

Rishikesh

Far away from any urban area, Rishikesh, India, is a small town located at the foothills of the Himalayas where the River Ganges flows out into the plains. The Maharishi's meditation academy was perched up on the side of a hill with a beautiful view overlooking the town and the plains for miles. The place was like a summer camp in the country with a row of little bungalows set up around the compound where students slept and meditated in private and a main building where they ate and listened to lectures by the Maharishi. People from all over the world attended the academy to become proficient at the Maharishi's method of meditation so that they could pass on the knowledge and experience to others.

In February 1968, the Beatles, their wives and some friends left for their three-month retreat at the Maharishi's meditation academy. While John, Paul, and George carried their acoustic guitars, Ringo had a suitcase full of Heinz Beans. His allergies prevented him from eating a variety of foods and the spicy Indian food would be too much for his delicate stomach. When the Beatles arrived at the New Delhi airport, a barrage of reporters confronted them. Once they reached Rishikesh, located several hours away, they found themselves secluded from the rest of the world.

Several celebrities were in attendance, including Mike Love of the Beach Boys and actress Mia Farrow. Everyone was outfitted with tailor-made Indian clothing. The women wore saris, which are made of a colorful lightweight cloth with one end wrapped about the waist to form a skirt and the other draped over the shoulder or covering the head. Most of the men wore lightweight loose cotton shirts and trousers. The weather was perfect with warm sunny days and cool nights. The routine was fairly simple and just required meditation a couple of times a day. Everyone set his or her own time limits for meditation. There was plenty of free time to relax and socialize. Occasionally, the Maharishi gave lectures and often met with students in small groups.

During their free time, John, Paul and George wrote and practiced songs on their acoustic guitars. George had also brought a sitar. Most of these songs ended up on their next album. They felt very comfortable without the stress of everyday life and were pleased with by all the natural beauty that surrounded them. There was wildlife inside and outside the compound. Wild monkeys would frequently sneak up by the outdoor food area and take off with some bread.

Ringo and Maureen decided to leave within a couple of weeks of their arrival. They said they missed their children and were satisfied with their meditation experience, but it wasn't something they were too serious about. A month later, Paul also decided to leave. He felt he had learned what he needed to know and was also very pleased with his time there. John and George, however, planned to stay until the end of the session. Several weeks later, when rumors of improper behavior by Maharishi surfaced, John and George were very dismayed and left quite quickly. Despite the abrupt ending, they were very pleased with their overall experience in Rishikesh as it gave them an opportunity to relax away from the hustle and bustle of daily life. They still endorsed meditation as an excellent way to spiritual enlightenment.

Beatle Bits

Paul Saltzman, a young Canadian in his mid-twenties, happened to be in India at this time. He attended a lecture by the Maharishi in New Delhi and was very intrigued by his message. Saltzman made his way to Rishikesh not knowing that the Beatles were there. The officials wouldn't allow him in as the academy was closed to visitors. After a week of camping outside the compound they saw that he was very serious about meditation, so they let him attend. He was thrilled to see the Beatles and was able to spend some time with them, not just as a fan, but also as a fellow student. He frequently watched them practice new songs. He took several photographs, but it wasn't until thirty years later he published a book about his experience there along with the amazing photographs he took in Rishikesh.

The Beatles, Maharishi (center) and other guests pose for a photo in Rishikesh, India.

Copyright Paul Saltzman.

Crowds gather outside Apple Boutique.

An Apple a Day Keeps the Taxman Away

The Beatles were advised to invest their money in business ventures in order to avoid continuing to pay very high taxes on their earnings. Prior to Brian's death, he had set up a company that eventually became Apple Corps with several subsidiaries such as Apple Films, Apple Publishing, Apple Retail, and Apple Records. They wanted to use these companies not only for their own creative projects, but for other artists as well. John and Paul, who were the primary driving forces behind these ideas, even went to New York and held a press conference to announce the creation of the company. They said that any artist who wanted to make a film, record or engage in other creative ventures wouldn't have to go and beg other companies to get it done. Instead, one of the Apple companies would try and help their dreams come true. The Beatles hired some staff to look after all these things so that the group could continue with their own creative endeavors.

Needless to say, the response to this generous offer was tremendous and Apple was overwhelmed with requests for money for music, films, books, and a number of other creative ventures. The offices were inundated with tapes, manuscripts, film scripts, and several other items. The Apple offices were open to the public, so many brought their ideas in person and left with some money to pursue their project.

One area of Apple the Beatles took personal interest in was, not surprisingly, music. They even wrote some songs for other artists to sing specifically under the new company label. Artists were also encouraged to develop their own material. Among the artists launched into successful careers with the help of Apple were James Taylor, Badfinger, and Billy Preston.

The Beatles also liked the idea of a store that would sell a variety of 'beautiful things' like stylish clothing, psychedelic furniture, small musical instruments, exotic jewelry, and paintings for low prices. They opened a store called "Apple Boutique" with the building painted in psychedelic colors. It violated some building codes, however, and ended being repainted white. The store lost a lot of money and even though the Beatles were not directly involved in managing the store, issues relating to the store became a distraction for them and they decided to shut it down in the summer of 1968. Rather than sell off the inventory, they decided to give it all away to the public for free. That created quite a commotion and required the police to control the crowds. The Beatles knew that despite their best intentions, they weren't businessmen and needed professional management of the Apple group of companies. They began to search for a professional manager.

Take a Sad Song and Make It Better

It was apparent to everyone around the Beatles that John's marriage to Cynthia wasn't going well. He had met and married her before Beatlemania took hold, and since then the pressure of being a Beatle and the time spent away from her, especially during the early days of their marriage, affected their relationship. Although Cynthia often accompanied John on trips, she spent the rest of her time taking care of their son, Julian. Then in late 1966, John met another woman, Yoko Ono. She was an unconventional artist and John found that he had a lot in common with her. By early 1968, John decided to end his marriage with Cynthia and begin a life with Yoko.

Paul was concerned about the effect of the break-up on Julian, who was a little over four at that time. Paul was close to Julian and was like an uncle to him. On his way to visit and give his support to Cynthia and Julian, he contemplated what he would say to Julian. The words he came up with to console Julian became the lyrics to his next single, "Hey Jude," and Paul dedicated the song to Julian. Originally Paul wrote "Jools," Julian's nickname, but changed it to "Jude" because it was easier to sing. The song ended up being about seven minutes long and required some very clever engineering to fit that much time into one single. At that time, it was the longest single ever recorded. Many in the music industry were very skeptical about releasing such a long single and doubted if many radio stations would even play the song. Not only did it reach number one when it was released in the summer of 1968, it became the all time best-selling single for the Beatles.

On the flip side of "Hey Jude" was John's fast rocking "Revolution." It was originally a slow song, but the other Beatles felt it would be better if it were faster. They decided to put the slow version on their next album. In

"Revolution," John was advocating peaceful change because violent protests were replacing peaceful protests used in the past. The Beatles were increasingly speaking out against all the violence in the world.

Sea of Holes

The Beatles were still contractually obligated to make a third full-length feature film, but were not interested in spending the time to make one. Due to the success of the cartoon series on American television, they agreed to an animated film called *Yellow Submarine*, which was the title of a song they had released previously. Although the scriptwriters got some ideas from the Beatles, most of the movie was completed without much involvement by the Beatles. The Beatles liked the underlying theme of the movie, which promotes peace and love. In the confrontations with the enemy, no one is killed or hurt, instead, music is used to turn the enemy into peace-loving creatures. The movie opened in the summer of 1968 to mixed reviews by the critics, but was loved by kids of all ages.

Although there were sixteen Beatles songs in the movie, only four of them were new. The Beatles were busy with their own creative projects and didn't have much time to record new songs. George wrote two of the four new songs, "Only a Northern Song" and "It's All Too Much." They reflected his dissatisfaction with the Beatles business dealings and the pressures of being a Beatle. They were written and recorded in early to mid-1967, prior to meeting the Maharishi and the trip to India. Paul's "All Together Now" and John's "Hey Bulldog" were fairly simple and fun songs. It was rumored that 'bulldog' was not in the original lyrics, but was 'bullfrog' instead. During rehearsals, Paul was joking around and barked at the end of the song, so it was changed to bulldog. A reference to bullfrog is still in the song. Previously released "All You Need is Love" and "Yellow Submarine" were added to the four new songs in the album. The rest of the album was George Martin's orchestral movie score.

The release was delayed until January 1969 in order to avoid a conflict with their next album. Many fans were disappointed because there were only four new songs instead of the usual twelve to fourteen. In 1999, a complete soundtrack with all the songs that were in the movie was released without the orchestral movie score. A DVD of the movie that included previously cut scenes was also released.

Beatle Bits

Just before the Beatles left for India, they recorded "Lady Madonna" and "Inner Light," which were released as a single while they were in India. Paul wrote "Lady Madonna" as a tribute to working-class women, particularly highlighting the difficulty of motherhood. George's "The Inner Light" was another one of his spiritual Indian songs using the sitar and Indian musicians.

Take a look back at the "Beatle Bits" on page 101. Don't you think it was quite an extraordinary coincidence that the man who gave George a book on yoga was from Rishikesh, India? The incident becomes even more astonishing considering that this took place in the Bahamas, thousands of miles away from both India and Britain!

Above: Front cover of the original *Yellow Submarine* album.

Below: The original *Yellow Submarine* album song list.

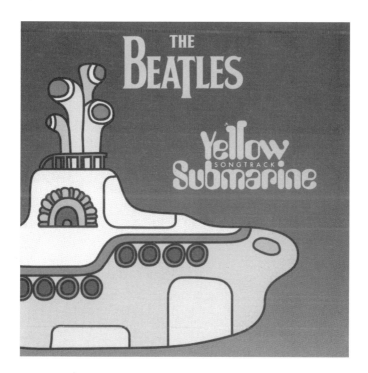

Above: Front cover of the re-issued *Yellow Submarine* album.

Below: The re-issued *Yellow Submarine* album song list.

1. Yellow Submarine
2. Hey Bulldog
3. Eleanor Rigby
4. Love You To
5. All Together Now
6. Lucy In The Sky With Diamonds
7. Think For Yourself
8. Sgt. Pepper's Lonely Hearts Club Band
9. With A Little Help From My Friends
10. Baby You're A Rich Man
11. Only A Northern Song
12. All You Need Is Love
13. When I'm Sixty Four
14. Nowhere Man
15. It's All Too Much

CDP 7243 5 21481 2 7

All tracks remixed at Abbey Road Studios.
Remix engineer Peter Cobbin assisted by Paul Hicks and Mirek Stiles.
Project co-ordinator Allan Rouse. Thanks to Peter Mew and Steve Rooke.
Original engineers Geoff Emerick (Except where noted otherwise)
Norman Smith tracks 7 & 14, Keith Grant track 10,
Dave Siddle track 15, Geoff Emerick and Eddie Kramer track 12
℗ 1999 The copyright in this sound recording is owned by EMI Records Ltd. © 1999 Subafilms Ltd.
"Yellow Submarine" and ~ Trademark of Subafilms Ltd. © 1999 EMI Records Ltd.
Manufactured by Capitol Records, Inc. Printed in U.S.A.

11

I, Me, Mine

White and Whiter

While the Beatles were in India, they spent a lot of time composing and practicing new songs. In addition, they had written songs before and after their trip to India; consequently they had accumulated a lot of new material. George had at least four he wanted on the album with Paul and John having at least a dozen or so each, and Ringo had written a song for the first time. They debated what to do. None of them wanted to give up many of their songs. George Martin pushed for one very good album; he thought many of songs were average. Rather than selecting what would be included in their next album, they decided to include most of them, resulting in a double album. Even then there were several left for future albums. The result was an album with a tremendous amount of variety.

The album was simply titled *The Beatles* and the cover was plain white, so it was nicknamed, the *White Album*. "The Beatles" was simply embossed on the cover. (Compact disc editions have "The Beatles" in gray). Furthermore, most of the recordings were produced using very few advanced studio techniques. Since there was so much material and a deadline approaching, there were occasions when three studios were being used at the same time, so that John, Paul, and George could each spend the time they needed to work on their own material. This album marked quite a significant change from the extravagant and very sophisticated *Sgt. Pepper's Lonely Hearts Club Band* and the colorful and whimsical *Magical Mystery Tour* albums.

Despite the substantial shift in design and the simple recording techniques, the eclectic album topped the charts when it was released in November 1968, the first double album to reach number one in pop music. As expected, it received mixed reviews from fans and critics. Many fans consider this album as their favorite while others wished the Beatles had selected the best songs and made it just one album. Other fans wanted two separate albums. Ringo jumped into the debate and joked, "I agree that we should have put it out as two separate albums: the 'White' and the 'Whiter' albums."

George probably made the biggest impression on the album with "While My Guitar Gently Weeps," revealing a vast improvement in his songwriting. He brought in his friend, Eric Clapton, to play lead guitar on the song. George made fun of Eric's fondness for chocolates in "Savoy Truffle." Ringo's "Don't Pass Me By" was written in 1964 as a country and western song and was finally polished off for the *White Album*. A violinist was brought in to give it a true country and western feeling. Ringo also sang on John's "Good Night," a bedtime lullaby that John had written for Julian shortly before his divorce.

Inspired by actress Mia Farrow's younger sister, Prudence, John wrote "Dear Prudence" to entice her to come out and join the others because she meditated for extended periods and rarely came out of her bungalow. When "Lucy in the Sky with Diamonds" was released a couple of years ago, people thought the song title was meant to be an acronym for a drug. Since then, Beatles fans and foes, were always looking for hidden meanings and clues in their songs. John wrote "Glass Onion" with the intent of providing a lot of hidden meanings and clues just for fun. On the serious side, John wrote "Julia" as a tribute to his late mother.

"Back in the USSR" was a parody of "Back in the USA" by Chuck Berry and "California Girls" by the Beach Boys. USSR stood for Union of Soviet Socialist Republics, a communist state leading the cold war against countries in the west like the United States and those of Western Europe. When Paul played a bit of it at Rishikesh, Mike Love of the Beach Boys suggested using Russian girls in the song. The Beatles did get criticized about the song, as some believed they were promoting communism.

Paul knew a Nigerian conga (drums) player who frequently used the expression "Ob la di, ob la da, life goes on." Paul used it as the basis for "Ob La Di, Ob La Da," a simple song with a touch of reggae music, about a day in the life of a young couple, Desmond and Molly Jones. There was a mistake in the song where Paul says that Desmond puts on make-up, instead of Molly, but they decided to leave it in. Paul's concern for civil rights in America inspired "Blackbird." It was a tribute to black women, encouraging them to keep their faith. "Bird" is slang for woman in Britain.

The BEATLES

Above: Front cover of *The Beatles*, also known as the *White album*.

Below: Back cover of the *White album*

The *White album* song list.

Five of Us

Since the death of Brian year before, the Beatles had found themselves frequently at odds with each other on business decisions, creative direction, and increasingly in recording issues in the studio. Their personal lives had been taking more precedence. Ringo enjoyed spending time with Maureen and his kids. George and Pattie were increasingly immersing themselves with Indian spirituality and he was getting disgruntled being constrained creatively as a Beatle. John was in the process of divorcing Cynthia and had started seeing Yoko. Paul, the only bachelor, was having his own relationship issues. He was trying to court a new woman he met, Linda Eastman. Each one of them was also increasingly pursuing their own creative interests in movies, music, and art.

The Beatles and Yoko Ono listening to a playback of a song in the studio.

Despite the simplicity of the songs on the *White Album*, it took nearly five months to record. In addition to outside pressures and distractions, the internal tensions between each member during the recordings sessions were mounting. Small problems that would have been overlooked in the past became big. John and Yoko had become inseparable and he brought her to the studio, adding to the tension. Normal protocol for visitors was to remain in the control room during recording sessions, but Yoko stayed very close to John. For the first time, it wasn't just the four of them in the studio. The atmosphere had become very uncomfortable and everyone was quite edgy. When Yoko was sick, a bed was brought into the studio for her to rest. Although other wives occasionally participated in background vocals, Yoko actually got her own lines in some of John's songs. The other Beatles weren't very pleased.

Three months of constant bickering finally got to Ringo and he quit the group. He also felt the other three weren't happy with his work. Ringo found out that he wasn't alone in that feeling. Each of the other band members had the same concern. Ringo took off on vacation to the Mediterranean Sea to unwind on a friend's yacht. John, Paul, and George sent him a telegram telling him they loved him and that he was the best drummer in the world and to please come back. Ringo came back after a couple of weeks and got a huge "welcome back" with the studio decked out with tons of flowers. After his return, the atmosphere improved for the rest of the recording sessions as they put the finishing touches to the album. The strain of spending months recording the *White Album*, along with other personal pressures, had begun to affect their relationships with each other.

A Rooftop Full of Noise

Shortly after completing the *White Album*, Paul suggested that perhaps the group could be rejuvenated if they played live to an audience again as they did in the early days. None of the others wanted to go on tour, but reluctantly agreed to perform live for one concert with completely new material and have an album made of their live performance. Therefore, the songs would have to be simple to be played live. They also agreed to film a documentary for television about their preparations and rehearsals for the concert and the concert itself. Ideas for the location of the concert were quite varied and ranged from Sahara Desert to a cruise ship to smaller locations in England. They couldn't decide on the location, but did agree that they had to start rehearsals and filming quickly due to the limited availability of the movie studio.

They began rehearsing and filming in early January 1969 at Twickenham Film Studios. These sessions were referred to as the "Get Back" sessions. Everyone hoped that the New Year would bring about a fresh new start, but it was not to be. With the cameras rolling, it wasn't long before the squabbling began again. The first problem they faced was that they had to start rehearsing at eight in the morning in order to keep regular hours for the film crew. Normally, they would come to the recording studio late in the morning or early afternoon and work late into the night. They found it difficult to get motivated and be creative early in the morning. Then there was the cold atmosphere of the film studio. It was an inhospitable, enormous, open barn-like building, lacking the coziness of the recording studio, with the added intrusion of cameras all around them while they tried to carry on as normal. To add to the tension, Yoko remained beside John at all times. Unlike most of the *White Album* where they had several individual recording sessions, this was a big jamming session with everyone involved at the same time in preparation for the concert. Unfortunately, the documentary of them rehearsing and preparing for a concert turned out to be a documentary on their troubles instead.

After a couple of weeks of rehearsing, George was not happy with the infighting and left for lunch and did not return. He stayed away for several days. They asked him to meet with them to discuss their problems. George told them he would return on the condition that they didn't rehearse at the film studios and abandon the idea of a live concert. He just wanted to go back to Abbey Road Studios and record an album. They agreed and decided that even though they weren't going to play live, they would simply play and record just as you would in a concert and make a simple album without using many studio techniques.

During the *White Album* sessions, George had

The rooftop concert.

brought in his friend Eric Clapton to play on "While My Guitar Gently Weeps." He found that when Eric was in the studio, the atmosphere improved a lot, like having a visitor at home and everyone seems to behave better. George invited another friend, Billy Preston, an American keyboard player to join in on some of the sessions. The Beatles had met Billy in Hamburg in 1962 and had remained friends ever since. Immediately, everyone's mood improved. Returning to the friendly and comfortable environment of the Abbey Road Studios also helped.

The filming continued in the studio. When they were getting close to finishing the album, they decided after much debate, that they would play live on the rooftop of their building to give the documentary a good ending and also just to have fun. It was a five-story office building adjoined with other buildings with a flat roof in a very busy London commercial district.

About mid-day on January 30, 1969, the Beatles played live on the rooftop. It would be their last live performance ever. Traffic was brought to a halt as office workers, shoppers, and others stopped and wondered what was going on as they looked up on that chilly January afternoon. Crowds began to gather on the street. They could barely see people on the rooftop from the street, but could certainly hear the music. Many people went to the rooftops of other buildings, while others peered from the windows trying to get a glimpse. The police arrived to control the crowds and entered the building. Officers made their way up to the roof and asked the Beatles to stop, but the band refused and continued playing. After some discussion with the staff, the police cut the power off and the concert ended, but not until the Beatles had a chance to play several songs and had a great time doing it. It was quite ironic that they established themselves in the cellars of Liverpool and performed for the last time on a rooftop in London.

Let It Be or *Let It Be...Naked*?

While the film was being edited, the recordings for this album were put away. None of the Beatles were too pleased with the way their songs had turned out and were not too interested in spending any more time on working on the album, as there were already a lot of hours of recordings to shift through. It wasn't until several months later that another producer, Phil Spector, was asked to produce the album, which was now titled *Let It Be*. His involvement was controversial because it was the first time George Martin had not produced a Beatle album. Also, Phil decided to add some studio techniques and orchestral back-up on some of the songs, which didn't please Paul, though the other Beatles were fine with it. Paul was particularly incensed about the orchestral back-up on "The Long and Winding

Road." Therefore in 2003, Paul released *Let It Be...Naked*. The album was a remake of the original recordings without adding much in studio effects and a change to the order of the songs, which Paul believed was the way the Beatles had originally intended.

Sometime during the tense period of the stormy recording sessions, Paul had a dream about his late mother, Mary, advising him that everything would be all right. The dream was the inspiration to the song "Let It Be." Paul and Linda had been spending a lot of time together and in "Two of Us" he wrote about their trips to the countryside, sometimes just getting lost in the middle of nowhere. George's discovery of Indian spirituality led him to examine his own life and in "I, Me, Mine," he takes a dim view of people's preoccupation with their own egos and demands. George felt that people were very demanding, but not very giving. "*I* am this," "Give it to *me*," or "This is *mine*," are examples of the selfishness that he despised. Perhaps he was also making a comment on the reasons why the Beatles were having problems.

"Across the Universe" was originally recorded in early 1968 and was donated for use on a charity album to benefit the World Wildlife Fund. On that version, the sound of birds chirping and flying away was added at the beginning of the song. Two of the Apple Scruffs' teenaged girls were brought in to sing in the background. In the *Let It Be* version their voices were not included and an orchestra was added instead. The original version with the birds and girls can be heard on the *Past Masters, Volume Two* compact disc. "One After 909" was one of the first collaborations by John and Paul and was originally recorded in 1963 for the Decca records audition, but had never found a place in an album until it was recorded again for *Let It Be*. The Beatles always enjoyed playing it live and did so on the rooftop.

Beatle Bits

Apple Scruffs

A group of fans regularly gathered outside Abbey Road Studios to catch a glimpse of the Beatles. Regardless of the weather, some would wait late into the night, sometimes all night, until the Beatles emerged from their recording sessions. They were there so often that eventually, the Beatles got to know a few by name. One of them even walked Paul's dog occasionally. They formed a fan club of their own and even published a magazine. They were nicknamed "Apple Scruffs." They were even honored by George who wrote a song about them called "Apple Scruffs."

Christmas Records

The Beatles were deluged with fan mail even before Beatlemania caught on nationally. Since the numbers were overwhelming, they were unable to keep up and respond on a timely basis. They agreed to record a Christmas message on a record and send it to members of the Beatles Fan Club at no charge. They included a special newsletter. They continued to do this every Christmas from 1963 until 1969. These recordings not only featured Christmas songs by the Beatles, but also included entertaining ad-libs and banter between the Beatles. Drawings by Julian Lennon and Zak Starkey, John's and Ringo's sons respectively, were used on the cover of a couple of Christmas records.

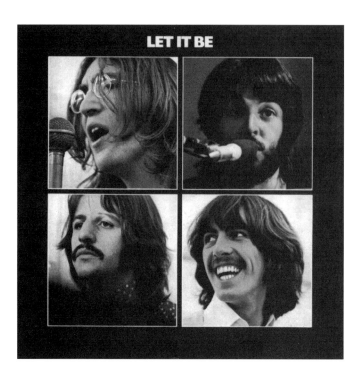

Above: Front cover of the original *Let It Be* album

Below: The original *Let It Be* album song list.

Above: Front cover of the re-issued *Let It Be* album.

Below: The re-issued *Let It Be* album song list.

Paul with his new bride, Linda.

12

Farewells Are Only Beginnings

Bed Peace, Hair Peace

There were many broken hearted teenaged girls around the world on March 12, 1969, when Paul finally married Linda in a very simple ceremony as hundreds of fans gathered outside to celebrate with them. Many of the teenaged female fans wept openly to lament losing the last bachelor Beatle. A couple of weeks later, John and Yoko left for Europe to get married. They planned to get married by the captain of the cross channel ferry that transported people across the English Channel to France. They weren't able to board due to lack of proper documentation. Then they found out the captain didn't preside over weddings anymore, so they flew to Paris and hoped to get married

John with his new bride, Yoko.

John and Yoko talk to reporters during their bed-in for peace campaign.

there. Unfortunately, they didn't meet minimum residency requirements. After making inquires about getting married in other European countries, they ended up getting married in Gibraltar, a British-governed island in the Mediterranean Sea.

John and Yoko returned to Paris before going on to Amsterdam to begin a week-long "bed-in for peace" campaign. They stayed in bed for a week at the Amsterdam Hilton Hotel and invited the press to visit them. John and Yoko felt that since the press constantly reported on everything they did, they might as well promote peace through the press. Their plan worked and they made the news around the world although not all of it was favorable, especially by the British press.

"The Ballad of John and Yoko" was a song written by John about his experience trying to get married and the "bed-in for peace" campaign. John was eager to record it as soon as he returned to London, but George and Ringo weren't available. He and Paul decided to go ahead and record it with just the two of them. By overdubbing, they were able to play different instruments on the song. The song was released as a single along with George's "Old Brown Shoe," another spiritually inspired song.

John and Yoko repeated the bed-in for peace in Montreal in May and generated even more publicity, as the North American press was still quite partial to the Beatles. During their stay, John wrote and recorded "Give Peace a Chance" in the hotel room with several visitors participating in the chorus. The song became a popular anti-war song for peace activists and is still used today to promote peace. Although this song was credited to Lennon/McCartney, it was released as a Plastic Ono Band song. John had formed the Plastic Ono Band to give Yoko and he an outlet for their joint musical creations.

Final Crossing

Wanting to put the difficulties of the recent recording sessions behind them, the Beatles decided to record another album, but this time with no gimmicks. George Martin was quite apprehensive about working with them again because of the recent stressful recording sessions, but they convinced him that they were willing to work together like in the good old days. The recording sessions went very well, perhaps because they subconsciously knew this might be their last album.

Yoko remained in the studio next to John, but the other Beatles had conceded that they were inseparable and did not dwell on it. A couple of months into the recording sessions, John and Yoko were in a car accident. Fortunately they weren't seriously injured, although they were hospitalized for a few days. Yoko needed a bit more time for recovery, so a bed was brought into the studio for her. The album was completed by late August. The cover photo for the album showed them crossing Abbey Road using a pedestrian crosswalk just outside the studio. That photo has been one of the most parodied album covers ever. They decided to call the album simply *Abbey Road* as a tribute to the recording studio they had called home for so many years. It was the last album they recorded together. *Abbey Road* was released in late September 1969 and quickly reached the top of the charts around the world and became one of their best-selling albums. Many fans consider it their favorite album.

George's songwriting shone on this album with "Something," a beautiful love song he wrote for Pattie. "Something" was released as a single and reached number one, marking the first time George's song was on the A side of a single. Ray Charles, Elvis Presley, and Frank Sinatra were among many artists who covered the song, making it the second-most Beatles song covered by other artists, with "Yesterday" holding the top honors. "Here Comes the Sun" was another excellent song by George, which was written while he walked around Eric Clapton's garden enjoying the sunshine on a pleasant early spring day.

Ringo wrote "Octopus's Garden" while he was on a yacht in the Mediterranean Sea during the time he temporarily quit the Beatles during the *White Album* sessions. The captain told him about the lives of octopuses in the sea and Ringo turned it into a song enjoyed by kids of all ages. A California politician, whose slogan was "Come Together," asked John to write a campaign song for him. John wrote "Come Together," but didn't think it was suitable for the campaign and ended up recording it for *Abbey Road*. It was released as the B side to "Something." A piece by Beethoven inspired John to write "Because," a complicated and intricate three-part harmony requiring John, Paul, and George to sing together. George Martin overdubbed the harmony three times to give the effect of nine voices.

Over the years, the Beatles had a difficult time

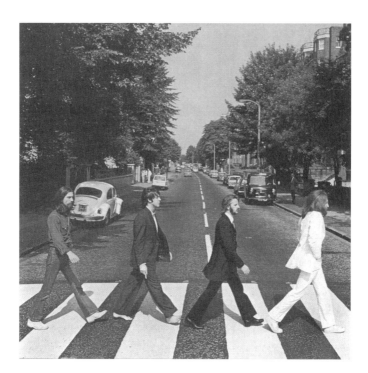

Above: Front cover of *Abbey Road*.

Below: *Abbey Road* song list.

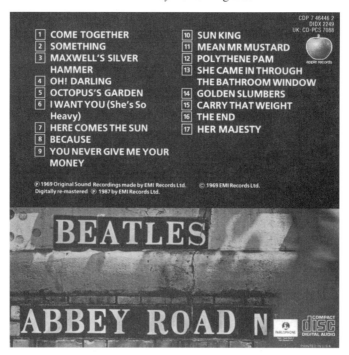

managing and understanding their finances. They were frustrated with the responses they got and never quite grasped the convoluted financial information they were given. They preferred to see their money in cash, so when they got papers full of financial information, they called them "funny paper." Paul's frustration with this is revealed in "You Never Give Me Your Money." Although they appreciated the Apple scruffs, occasionally they had some problems with them. On one occasion, some had broken in Paul's home and taken several small items like photographs. Other Apple scruffs managed to retrieve most of the items and return them to Paul. This event inspired Paul to write "She Came in Through the Bathroom Window."

Perhaps the most intriguing part of the album is the spirited sixteen-minute medley that takes you seamlessly through eight songs, some quite brief, starting from "You Never Give Me Your Money" to "The End." John, Paul, and George each took a turn at a brief guitar solo while Ringo performed his first ever drum solo on "The End." "The End" climaxes with one of the most quoted Beatles lines: "And in the end, the love you take is equal to the love you make." This turned out to be a very fitting ending to their last song on their last, and perhaps, their best album.

"I Hope We Passed the Audition"

Shortly after completion of *Abbey Road*, the Plastic Ono Band gave a short live performance at a peace festival in Toronto in September 1969. John's live performance without the rest of the Beatles increased the speculation about them breaking up, but the band kept denying it. After John's return, Paul brought up the idea of going back to their roots and playing in small clubs because that's what they really enjoyed. John told them, however, that he had decided to leave the group. John's disclosure was a surprise,

DAILY Mirror

5d. Friday, April 10, 1970   No. 20,616

Lennon-McCartney song team splits up

PAUL IS QUITTING THE BEATLES

Swing to Labour .. but Tories are still in command

LABOUR scored morale-boosting gains in the Greater London Council elections early today—but the swing was not nearly enough to wrest control from the Tories.

They captured three seats from the Tories at Camden—and one at Greenwich.

First results showed an average swing to Labour of just over 3 per cent, compared with 1967, when the seats were last contested.

By VICTOR KNIGHT

At 2 a.m. it was still doubtful whether Labour would be able to gain the eleven seats needed to win control of the Inner London Education Authority.

But there was no doubt that they would not be able to gain the 57 seats necessary to control the Greater London Council itself.

Hampered

Date

Counts

By DON SHORT

PAUL McCARTNEY has quit the Beatles. The shock news must mean the end of Britain's most famous pop group, which has been idolised by millions the world over for nearly ten years.

Today 27-year-old McCartney will announce his decision, and the reasons for it, in a no-holds-barred statement.

McCartney . . . a policy deadlock.

Clash over the running of Apple

Films

but not a shock to the others, after all, George and Ringo had also quit and then returned in the not-so-distant-past. This time, however, they knew it was for real. They agreed to keep it amongst themselves until some of the business matters that were ongoing were sorted out.

As they had done in the recent past, they continued working on their own artistic projects including their own solo singles and albums. In December, *The Plastic Ono Band - Live Peace in Toronto* album was released. In February, the Plastic Ono Band released a new single "Instant Karma." Ringo planned to release *Sentimental Journey* in March. Paul planned to release, *McCartney* in mid-April. The rest of the group, however, wanted Paul to delay his album because it was too close to the date when the *Let It Be* movie and album would be released. They ended up delaying *Let It Be* instead.

Paul did not want to do any interviews prior to releasing *McCartney,* so he included a question and answer page in his press release. He asked Apple's press secretary, Peter Brown, to ask any questions that the press would normally ask and Paul said he would respond honestly. To the question, "Do you foresee a time when Lennon/McCartney becomes an active songwriting partnership again?" Paul responded, "No." The break-up of the Beatles was now public knowledge and made headlines around the world. Since it was Paul who put out the press release, many believed that Paul was the first to quit.

The album and movie *Let It Be* were released in May 1970. The album received mixed reviews, but still topped the charts. The movie let the fans to see some of the problems the Beatles had been having and the final live performance on the rooftop of Abbey Road Studios. At the end of the brief concert, John quips, "I'd like to say thank you on behalf of the group and ourselves and I hope we passed the audition."

Backstage

A lot of fans were quick to point the blame at Yoko as the impetus behind the Beatles break-up asserting that her influence on John took him away from the Beatles. Others accused Linda of doing the same to Paul. Each Beatle was blamed for one reason or another. Erroneous reporting by the media and by gossip publications just added to the confusion. Accusations were plentiful, but the truth was far more complicated.

Many fans forget that John, Paul, and George were just teenagers when they met and had been performing together since 1957. It wasn't until their dramatic rise in late 1963 in Britain and early 1964 in America that these fans first heard about them. By the time of their break-up in 1970, they had been together for nearly thirteen years, having spent a lot of time together. They were a very close-knit group, providing support for each other during trying times. The pressures of Beatlemania, the grueling touring schedule, frequent television and radio appearances, and the lack of privacy and control of their lives took a heavy toll on their lives. It wasn't just that they had become popular; it was the extraordinary scale of their fame, perhaps even still unmatched in history. Also keep in mind that they were only in their early twenties in 1964.

When they stopped touring, they had more freedom and opportunity to be more creative and pursue their own interests. It gave them a chance to grow up. They were able to balance their lives between the Beatles and their personal pursuits and still remain close to each other. Brian's death had a devastating effect on the Beatles, which wasn't quite evident at the time. He was their security blanket. Their complete reliance upon him to run their business affairs and their lack of business knowledge brought a whole new set of problems for them. Then they discovered that many of

Brian's business agreements were not always favorable to the benefit of the Beatles. Brian was a decent man, but not the astute businessman they thought he was. They found themselves in financial difficulties despite the incredible volume of record sales. They were frequently at odds with each other concerning the direction of their business ventures as well as their creative projects. It was at this time they slowly began to drift apart.

John and George were more interested in pursuing their own creative projects while Paul focused on the group's interests as evident by the *Sgt Pepper, Magical Mystery Tour* and *Let It Be* projects. Paul also tried to get the group to start performing live again, hoping it would bring back some of the spark of their early days. This caused some friction as Paul's assertiveness was misinterpreted as his attempt to become the leader of the group. George's keen interest in Indian spirituality and music took him in a different path from the rest of the group. George was also increasingly growing frustrated at the lack of opportunity to find room for his songs on the albums, especially as his writing was peaking around the time the group broke up. He had built up a sizeable library of new material by then. Unfortunately, he was in the unenviable position of having to compete with John and Paul who had started writing long before George did. They had established themselves as a formidable team, unmatched in pop culture. Ringo questioned his own role in the group, occasionally feeling like an outsider looking in. His interest in making movies was growing and taking him away from the music.

The arrival of Yoko into John's life complicated matters as he turned his attention to her. Her interests in avant-garde art and music appealed to John, who felt he had finally found his soul mate. Paul found his soul mate in Linda, who became his confidant as he found himself the only one opposing the changes in Apple's management. John, George, and Ringo supported a well-known entertainment manager, Allen Klein, to take over while Paul wanted Linda's father's law firm to handle the company's management. Allen took over control for a brief period.

It had become apparent early on in their career that anything one of them did, all of them had to answer for it. John's comments on Jesus were a prime example. By the late 1960s, being in the Beatles was stifling their individual creativity as they were constrained by having to be responsible to others for their own deeds. Having been together since their teens, they had not experienced freedom of being their own individuals. John and George were eager to move on and experience freedom of being on their own. Ringo was beginning to consider starting a new chapter in his life. In the end, Paul realized his own artistic endeavors were being inhibited and it would be best for all to move on. Despite some of the acrimony between them near the end, they continued to be friends and occasionally even played on each other's albums.

Much of this information wasn't readily available to fans in the early days, hence the misinterpretation of why they broke up. Still, beware that many myths and rumors abound, particularly on the Internet. Now, however, you are well prepared to question them. It is quite amazing to see what they accomplished despite the obstacles they faced. Whatever caused their break-up, it ended an era in pop culture and left behind a legacy that won't be forgotten for generations to come.

Beatle Bits

Will the Real Paul Stand Up?

Shortly after Abbey Road was released in the fall of 1969, a rumor that Paul had been killed in a car accident in 1966 and had been secretly replaced by a look-alike spread quickly around the world. The origin of this rumor is hard to pinpoint, but it was given some credibility when the media picked up the story. The Beatles, of course, denied it. This rumor went to another level when fans began to uncover dozens of "clues" from album covers and songs.

The most popular clue is the picture on the cover of *Abbey Road* of the Beatles crossing the road. Some fans believe this is actually a funeral procession. They say that John, dressed in white and leading the procession, symbolizes a priest followed by Ringo, dressed in black, as the undertaker. Paul, with bare feet, is the deceased, while George, in jeans, is the gravedigger. Several other clues were also identified on the cover. Other fans have discredited many of these clues.

Even *Life* magazine got in on the controversy and featured Paul on the cover with an accompanying article titled, "Paul is Still With Us." The "Paul is dead" controversy still lives on and fans still continue to debate the issue.

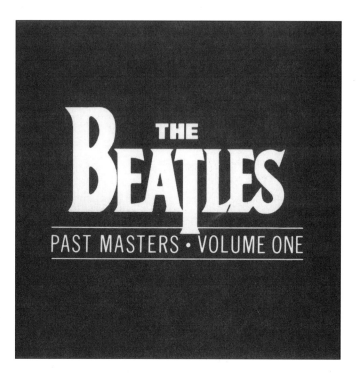

Above: Front cover of *Past Masters*, volume one.

Below: *Past Masters*, volume one song list.

Above: Front cover of *Past Masters*, volume two.

Below: *Past Masters*, volume two song list.

CDP 7 90044 2
DIDX 2889
STEREO except *MONO

COMPACT disc
DIGITAL AUDIO

1. DAY TRIPPER
2. WE CAN WORK IT OUT
3. PAPERBACK WRITER
4. RAIN
5. LADY MADONNA
6. THE INNER LIGHT
7. HEY JUDE
8. REVOLUTION
9. GET BACK (with Billy Preston)
10. DON'T LET ME DOWN1 (with Billy Preston)
11. THE BALLAD OF JOHN AND YOKO
12. OLD BROWN SHOE
13. ACROSS THE UNIVERSE
14. LET IT BE
15. *YOU KNOW MY NAME (LOOK UP THE NUMBER)

Produced by George Martin

Compilation by Mark Lewisohn.
Original Sound Recordings made by EMI Records Ltd.
This compilation ℗ 1988 EMI Records Ltd.
© 1988 EMI Records Ltd.
Printed in U.S.A.

PARLOPHONE

13

The Solo Years
A Brief Summary

John

With Yoko by his side, John continued to be outspoken about his views against the Vietnam War and campaigned for world peace. In December 1969, John and Yoko conveyed their Christmas message on billboards in several major cities around the world including New York, London, Tokyo, Rome, and Amsterdam. They proclaimed "War Is Over! If You Want It. Happy Christmas from John & Yoko." They also took out newspaper ads promoting the same message. Over the next couple of years they also wrote and released several songs with the anti-war and pro-peace theme. One of his most popular was "Imagine," which has become an anthem for world peace. John and Yoko also became quite active in their stance against Britain's involvement in Northern Ireland and campaigned for several other political causes.

In late 1971, John and Yoko moved to New York permanently. Over the next four years, John had to battle with the United States government to remain in the country. The government refused to give John permanent residency status and even attempted to deport him because he had a drug violation in Britain a few years earlier. John and Yoko, however, felt that it was politically motivated because of their anti-war stance as well their involvement in other political causes. Finally in 1975 the government dropped their case against John and he was allowed to remain in the United States.

After the Beatles disbanded, John was very active. He recorded and released several albums and singles with mixed results. The immigration battle had been very stressful. His political activism put Yoko and him in the media spotlight and the media attention wasn't always favorable. The legal battle over business affairs with the other Beatles had been very stressful and was finally resolved by the mid-1970s. His relationship with Yoko, who was expecting their child, had its own share of problems, which did, however, improve. John added 'Ono' to his middle name.

On John's thirty-fifth birthday, Yoko gave birth to Sean Ono Lennon. John decided to go on a hiatus for a while and stay home to help raise Sean. Later, John said he had felt guilty that he wasn't around much when Julian was growing up and hoped to make it up by being there for Sean. John hardly touched his guitar for nearly five years and then, in 1980, he felt the urge to go back to the recording studio and record an album. In October 1980,

Double Fantasy was released to critical and commercial success. John even considered going on tour.

On December 8, 1980, John and Yoko spent the day at the recording studio working on their next album. Later that evening, as they were entering the Dakota, their apartment building, John was shot and killed by a deranged man. John was only forty. Millions of fans around the world were shocked and mourned his death. Thousands of fans gathered outside the Dakota to comfort each other in this time of grief. John's funeral was a private ceremony attended by his closest friends and family. On the Sunday after his death, thousands of fans gathered in a ten-minute silent vigil in New York. An official memorial called Strawberry Fields was built in Central Park across the street from the Dakota. The centerpiece of the memorial is a circular mosaic on the ground with the word "Imagine" inscribed in the middle.

Over the years, Yoko has released several pieces of John's previously unreleased music. On October 9, 1990, John's fiftieth birthday was celebrated with a special simulcast of "Imagine" on more than 1,000 radio stations in over fifty countries, an unprecedented initiative sponsored by the United Nations. The city of Liverpool honored John by renaming the airport "Liverpool John Lennon Airport." Several other memorials are dedicated to John's memory around the world.

George

In the couple of years preceding the disbanding of the Beatles, George had been writing a lot of songs, but was unable to get many onto Beatles albums. So, it was no surprise that shortly after the break-up, he recorded and released *All Things Must Pass*, the first triple disc pop album. The album was a huge critical and commercial success, thrusting George out of the shadows of the Lennon/McCartney team, proving that he could succeed on his own.

"My Sweet Lord," a song from *All Things Must Pass*, was released as a single and was a huge hit. The publishers of "He's So Fine," however, sued him for plagiarism. They claimed that a melody in "My Sweet Lord" was similar to "He's So Fine," a hit in 1963. It was a very technical case and the court found "subconscious plagiarism," meaning it was unintentional. Nevertheless, George lost and although he wasn't pleased with the verdict, he decided to take a positive view of this situation and recorded "This Song," which made fun of the situation. *All Things Must Pass* was remastered digitally on compact disc in 2001 and included a revised version of "My Sweet Lord" without the melody in question.

George's Indian friend, Ravi Shankar, told George about the plight of the people of Bangladesh, formerly known as East Pakistan. Floods, famine, and war had devastated the country and Ravi asked George to help raise money for them. George organized two benefit concerts at Madison Square Gardens in New York in the summer of 1971 and asked several superstar performers to participate. Bob Dylan, Eric Clapton, Billy Preston, and Ringo Starr were among several who performed and helped raise several million dollars from concert revenue, donations, and sales of the resulting triple disc album, *Concert for Bangla Desh*. This event was the first event of its kind to raise money and awareness on a large scale for charity.

Over the next decade George recorded and released several albums and singles with mixed results. He divorced Pattie in the mid-1970s and married Olivia Arias. In 1978, George's only child, Dhani, was born. In the late 1980s George got together with Bob Dylan, Tom Petty, Roy Orbison, and Jeff Lynne and formed the Traveling

Wilburys. The group was formed just for fun and recorded and released two albums and a few singles. Unfortunately, Roy Orbison passed away after the first album. After the second album, they never got back together as they were just too busy with their own projects.

During the 1990s, George spent a lot of time collaborating with other artists rather than on his own work. He also worked with Paul and Ringo on *The Beatles Anthology.* (see "Anthology" section at the end of this chapter). The late nineties held unexpected difficulties for George. In 1997 George underwent surgery for throat and lung cancer, which could have been attributed to his smoking habit when he was younger. He then survived a knife attack by a mentally unstable person who broke into his home in Britain in 1999. It was revealed in mid-2001 that George was fighting brain cancer and was undergoing treatment in New York. On November 29, 2001, George passed away at a friend's home in Los Angeles. His wife, Olivia and son, Dhani were by his side.

Millions of his fans gathered in cities all over the world to mourn his death. Several memorials dedicated to George's memory have been put up around the world. A year after his death, Eric Clapton organized a special tribute concert for George in London. Paul, Ringo, Tom Petty, and Billy Preston were among several artists performing George's songs. George's son Dhani played the guitar. Ravi Shankar composed a special instrumental song, which was performed by a classical Indian orchestra and the London Symphony Orchestra.

Just prior to his death, George revealed that he was working on a new album, *Brainwashed*, that was nearly complete. Unfortunately, he passed away before he could finish it. Dhani and George's friend and producer, Jeff Lynne, produced it they way they felt George would have done. *Brainwashed* is among George's finest work.

Ringo

In the early 1970s Ringo had success with a string of singles, including "Photograph," which was co-written with George. John, Paul and George all contributed songs and worked with Ringo on his successful self-titled album and *Goodnight Vienna*. On *Ringo*, George, John and Ringo worked together on John's contribution "I'm the Greatest." This was the closest the former Beatles got to a reunion.

Ringo continued recording albums and singles until the early 1980s with mixed results. He also continued acting in movies. He divorced Maureen in the mid-1970s and later married Barbara Bach, an actress he met on a movie set. For most of the 1980s, Ringo stayed away from recording and performing. Then in 1989, he formed Ringo Starr and His All Starr Band made up of celebrities similar to George's Traveling Wilburys. The All Starr Band was specifically put together to go on tour with a varied cast of celebrities invited to participate in the different tours.

The All Starr Band has toured several times and featured celebrities like Billy Preston, Joe Walsh (the Eagles), Burton Cummings (the Guess Who), and John Entwistle (the Who). Ringo's son and accomplished drummer, Zak, also accompanied the band on a couple of tours. During this period, Ringo put out several successful albums. Some were compilations from the All Starr Band and others were his solo efforts. Ringo plans to continue touring with the All Starr Band. Ringo has three children: two boys, Zak and Jason, and a daughter, Lee.

Paul

After recording and releasing the highly successful *McCartney* and *Ram* albums, Paul and Linda, formed a band called, Paul McCartney and Wings, later just referred to as "Wings." Without much rehearsing, Wings performed at university campuses to the delight of the students. The first couple of Wings albums were moderately successful and then their next album, Band On The Run, was very successful. Over the next few years, Wings put out several number one albums and singles and toured the world to sold-out stadiums.

In 1980, Paul decided to go solo again and put out few more successful albums and singles in the early 1980s, but did not tour. Paul starred in a movie called Give My Regards to Broad Street in mid-1980s. The movie depicts a day in the life of a rock and roll star and featured several of his solo and Beatles songs. Linda, Ringo, and Barbara also had roles in the movie. It wasn't until 1989 that Paul returned with another fairly successful album and very successful world tour. Paul set a new world record for the largest stadium crowd in the history of popular music when he played to 184,000 in Brazil. In 1993, he set out on another very successful world tour.

Queen Elizabeth knighted Paul in 1996 for his contribution to music and he is now called Sir Paul McCartney. Two years later, fans all over the world mourned as Linda passed away from cancer. George and Ringo joined Paul and his children, Stella, Mary, and James, and stepdaughter, Heather, for Linda's memorial service in London. It was the first time in nearly thirty years that the three remaining Beatles were seen together in public. In 1999, Paul performed at the Cavern Club for the first time since the early days with the Beatles. 300 lucky fans won free tickets to see Paul perform.

Paul married Heather Mills in 2002. The following year, he embarked on one of his most successful world tours. Later that year, Paul and Heather's first child, Beatrice, was born. He continues releasing successful material and performing on very successful tours.

Above: Front cover of *Plastic Ono Band* album

Below: Front cover of *Imagine* album

Above: Front cover of *All Things Must Pass*

Below: Front cover of *Brainwashed*

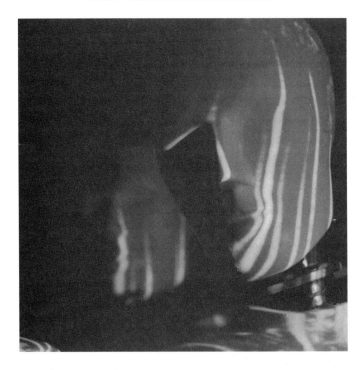

Above: Front cover of *Ringo*

Below: Front cover of *Vertical Man*

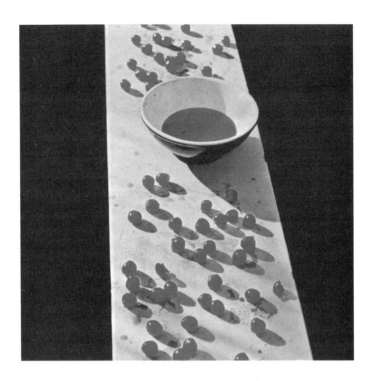

Above: Front cover of *McCartney*

Below: Front cover of *Ram*

The Anthology Project

After the break-up of the band, the Beatles discussed chronicling their history on film. The Beatles wanted their story told in their own words, but for one reason or another it was put off. Then in the early 1990s, the project finally got started. The project had expanded to include previously unreleased music and a detailed book. Neil Aspinall and Derek Taylor took on the massive task to sort through hundreds of hours of film. Paul, George, and Ringo were interviewed over the course of a few years. John's input was taken from interviews he had given. Some people who were close to the Beatles were also interviewed for the film. In the fall of 1995, a six-hour documentary, *The Beatles Anthology,* was shown on television around the world to an estimated audience of over 400 million people. The documentary is available on DVD with footage not seen on television.

George Martin took on the task of sorting through hundreds of hours of music and produced six compact discs with nearly 150 tracks in total. The result was a mix of studio outtakes, live performances, alternative versions, unreleased songs, and even private demo recordings in their conceptual stage. Perhaps the most significant result of *The Beatles Anthology* was the recording of "Free as a Bird" and "Real Love" by Paul, George and Ringo using John's low-quality demo recordings as the basis for the songs. Essentially, it was all four Beatles on the songs for the first time since they broke up. The compact discs were sold in sets of two over a period of one year. The first Anthology set broke single day record sales for albums in the United States and topped the charts. All three sets went to number one. It was the first time in thirty years that a band had three consecutive number one albums in America in a twelve-month period. The last band to do it, not surprisingly, was the Beatles. The covers consisted of a collage of photos and when the three covers are placed side by side, they create a single cover.

The book, with interviews and rare photographs was delayed for nearly four years and was finally released in 1999 and became a best-seller. Around the same time, a compilation of Beatles songs that had reached number one was released. *Beatles 1* was aimed at the younger generation of fans and quickly topped the charts in thirty-four countries. It became the fastest selling album ever, selling nearly 4 million copies in the first week. For the first time ever, a book and an album by the same artists were number one at the same time in the United States. It was no surprise that those artists were the Beatles, even though it was thirty years after their breakup.

Above: Front cover of *The Beatles Anthology I*

Above: Front cover of *The Beatles Anthology II*

Below: Front cover of *The Beatles Anthology III*

Afterword

Behind the Beatles Phenomenon

There's little doubt that the Beatles are one of the most popular music groups in pop culture history, but experts vary in their opinions of why the Beatles reached such extraordinary heights of fame. A few sociologists and psychologists suggest that the timing of the arrival of the Beatles on the music scene had a lot to do with it. They said that political scandals in Britain in the early 1960s combined with the death of president Kennedy in America left many youths feeling quite disillusioned. The Beatles, these experts said, provided the youth with an escape from their problems. Others say that the Beatles seemingly radical hairstyles combined with their charming personalities and the new sound struck a chord with the youth that other artists had not been able to reach in the past. Elvis had come the closest, but by the time the Beatles came on the scene, Elvis was focused on making movies.

Perhaps these explanations may be valid for the early days of Beatlemania, but the Beatles have continued to be popular long past the hysteria. It didn't take long for many bands to jump on the bandwagon to try and to look and sound like the Beatles. Other groups took a cue from the Beatles and began to write and record their own material, bringing another level of diversity to the music scene. While many of these artists achieved various levels of success, very few were able to come close to matching the success of the Beatles during the 1960s and even fewer were able to sustain their wide popularity in the long run. Pop/rock artists such as the Rolling Stones, the Who, Elvis and Eric Clapton are perhaps among a handful from the 1960s who remain popular today.

An explanation for the Beatles' longevity likely comes down to the variety in their large repertoire. From the early days in Hamburg and Liverpool and through to Abbey Road, the Beatles constantly experimented with a variety of music styles and brought fresh sounds to their fans. The Beatles were recognized as innovators and pioneers in pop music, but they also acknowledged learning from artists they admired when they were younger and from many of their contemporaries. There were many lesser-known artists whose innovations were not well known, but when the Beatles utilized those ideas, and usually improved upon them, they were credited for the innovation. It was a risky proposition for a band as popular as the Beatles to use new ideas because it risked alienating their fans. At the same time, they balanced the new with standard, simple songs. As a result, they gained more new fans than they lost and increased their appeal to an even wider audience.

The change in their style of music over the course of their career could be broken down into five eras:

The pre-Beatlemania years
Beatlemania years - *Please Please Me* to *Help!*
Studio years - *Rubber Soul* to *Sgt. Pepper*
The later years - *White Album* to *Abbey Road*
The solo years - after the break-up.

This division in style essentially makes the Beatles into four different bands and four individual solo performers. Some fans tend to identify with the Beatles in primarily one or two of these eras; others have a favorite Beatle or just a favorite album. Others, like me, enjoy the Beatles' entire spectrum of work. This diversity has led to a very varied and large group of fans around the world.

As a young fan, your perspective is quite different from the fans in the 1960s. You have the opportunity to pick and choose from the vast collection and assemble your own memories of the group. You will find that your music tastes will change as you get older and you will likely enjoy songs that don't interest you today. Hopefully, you will eventually come to appreciate the depth and the breadth of the complete Beatles repertoire for many years to come.

Beatle Bits

The Fifth Beatle

After Stuart Sutcliff stopped playing with the Beatles, they remained a quartet. Over the years fans have debated who should get the designation of the "fifth Beatle." The basis for this label is that the deserving person should be one whose presence had a substantial effect on their success and without that person, the Beatles as the world knew them, would not exist. These are very high standards to meet and there are many who played a vital role in the success of the group. Many different people have tried to call themselves or have been designated the "fifth Beatle" by fans or the media. There are only two people, however, whom I feel meet these standards. They are Brian Epstein, their manager and George Martin, their producer. Both men would easily qualify as they could each be considered "the glue that held the Beatles together." Their roles in the story of the Beatles were vital. Yet, they did this in a very different way and for very different reasons. Combine the contributions by both men and we have the ideal fifth Beatle.

A Little Help from their Friends

Jane Asher   Jane was Paul's former fiancée. They dated from 1963 until 1968. She generally kept out of the Beatles limelight and was focused on her career as a stage actress. Many of Paul's love songs the early years were inspired by Jane.

Neil Aspinall   Introduced to the Beatles by Pete Best, Neil started out as the Beatles' road manager and became a very close friend and confidant of the Beatles. After Brian's death, the Beatles relied on Neil to help them with their business affairs and he eventually became the head of Apple Corps.

Alf Bicknell   Alf was their chauffer and assistant from 1964 to 1966. He assisted them on their tours and was slightly hurt during the scuffle at Manila airport in the Philippines.

Peter Brown   Peter was Brian's assistant and after Brian's death, he worked at Apple Corps in various capacities.

Geoff Emerick   Geoff was a recording engineer and assisted George Martin with the production of several Beatles albums.

Mal Evans   Mal was a bouncer at the Cavern Club when the Beatles hired him to take over as road manager from Neil and became a close friend. After the Beatles stopped touring, he remained as their assistant.

Bill Harry   Bill attended the Liverpool College of Art with John Lennon, and founded *Mersey Beat*, a local music paper that frequently promoted the Beatles in the early days.

Richard Lester   Directed *A Hard Day's Night* and *Help!*.

Victor Spinetti   Acted in *A Hard Day's Night, Help!,* and *Magical Mystery Tour.*

Derek Taylor   Derek was a journalist and helped Brian write his autobiography, *A Cellarful of Noise*. He became Brian's assistant and later the Beatles' press officer.

Internet Resources

beatles.com The Beatles official website.

paulmccartney.com Paul McCartney's official website.

georgeharrison.com George Harrison's official website.

lennon.net The official website of the Liverpool Lennons.

ringostarr.com Ringo Starr's official website.

beatlefan.com Fan magazine.

daytrippin.com Online fan club and magazine.

beatlesfansunite.com Fan club and newsletter.

britishbeatlesfanclub.co.uk Fan club and magazine.

beatles-unlimited.com Fan magazine based in the Netherlands, but published in English. Also sponsors annual fan festival.

mersey-beat.net Online version of the original Liverpool entertainment paper still managed by Bill Harry.

brunchradio.com Weekly national radio show.

abbeyroadontheriver.com Annual fan festival.

thefestforbeatlesfans.com Annual fan festival.

liverpool.gov.uk City of Liverpool website.

teenbeatlesfans.com Official website for this book.

The Beatles in India

Photos by Paul Saltzman
905.901.1300
www.TheBeatlesInIndia.com

Imagine Love...

Albums, Songs, and Movies index

Key Beatles Events Index

General Index

General Index (Continued)

Selected Bibliography

Badman, Keith *The Beatles Off the Record* (Omnibus Press 2000)

Epstein, Brian *Cellarful of Noise* (Byron Press 1998)

Harrison, George, McCartney, Paul, Lennon, John, Starr, Ringo
    The Beatles Anthology (Chronicle Books 2000)

Harrison, George *I, Me, Mine* (Simon & Schuster 1980)

Harry, Bill *The Ultimate Beatles Encyclopedia* (Hyperion 1992)

Martin, George *All You Need is Ears* (Macmillan 1979)

Miles, Barry *The Beatles Diary* (Omnibus Press 1998)

Miles, Barry *Paul McCartney Many Years From Now* (Holt 1997)

Norman, Philip *Shout! The Beatles in their Generation*
    (Fireside 1981)

Saltzman, Paul *The Beatles in Rishikesh* (Viking Studio 2000)

Turner, Steve *A Hard Day's Write* (Carlton Books 1994)

Photo Credits

Mirror pix 12, 29, 39, 42, 44, 52, 54, 55, 59, 62, 68, 70, 74, 76, 84, 96
98, 103, 116, 124, 137, 138, 142, 145, 147, 167, 170, 176, 178, 184
Redferns Music Picture Library Ltd. 28, 31, 144, 155
Bill Harry/Mersey Beat Ltd. 36
Fairfax Photos 81
Paul Saltzman 154, 212
AP/World Wide Photos 86, 128, 179
New York Daily News 86, 106

Acknowledgements

Special thanks to my friends Alan Burggaller and Eloise Costello
for their encouragement, assistance and support.